# AMMU

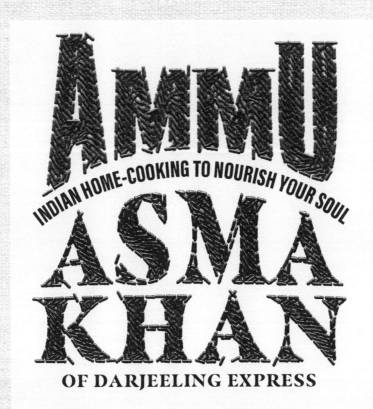

# AMMU

## INDIAN HOME-COOKING TO NOURISH YOUR SOUL

## ASMA KHAN

### OF DARJEELING EXPRESS

EBURY
PRESS

# DEDICATION

I heard Ammu's heartbeat even before I saw her face. I knew her voice and recognised her laughter even before she held me in her arms. Our deep bond began unseen by others, in the womb, and is the anchor of my life. This book celebrates the relationship between mother and daughter. It is a homage to my mother, who I call Ammu.

The picture opposite was taken at a family wedding when Ammu was five months pregnant. Everyone at the wedding told my mother how it looked as if she was carrying a boy. The heir to the family name. It was not a boy. It was me. The second daughter, who was going to grow up and become the heir to all of Ammu's recipes.

In this book, I celebrate a woman who is fiercely independent in her thinking, a woman ahead of her time, who managed to gently shake the patriarchy and was unafraid to be different from those around her, becoming a female founder of a food business. Ammu's footprints are too big for me to match them, but I am following her path and using food to celebrate my family's culinary heritage and culture. I also use food to change the narrative of how female cooks are perceived at home and in restaurant kitchens. I wrote this book to share the life lessons and recipes I have learned from Ammu. I want to pass on the legacy that I have inherited from Ammu to others.

Now, separated by oceans, I still feel Ammu's hand on me. Whenever I cook, in the aromas of the spices that infuse my kitchen, I feel her presence. When I was young, my father would tell me that heaven lay at the feet of my mother. I know it does. She is and will forever be my guiding light. My Ammu.

# CONTENTS

# INTRODUCTION

This book is a collection of recipes from my childhood. A celebration of where I come from, of home cooking, and the inextricable link between food and love. It is a chance for me to honour my *ammu* – my mother – and to share with you the recipes that made me and root me to home.

We have all lived through a challenging time, where many found solace in cooking. Unable to spend time with our families, many of us sought the food of our childhoods. The recipes and the memories I want to share – some sad, some happy – all possess something universal. Food is a way for us to have this conversation about how similar we all are – it connects us and unites us beyond differing appearances, accents, races and backgrounds. This book is a joyful celebration of memories of food and their power to heal. It is also an acknowledgement of the sacrifices parents make and the challenges they face while nurturing and feeding their children.

*Ammu* seems to be a combination of the word *amma*, which is widely used in South Asia to mean 'spiritual mother', and the Arabic word *umm*, also 'mother'. It is a term used mostly in South Asian Muslim homes for their mothers. I love that the term has the influence of different cultures, just like the food I grew up eating. I was lucky to have grown up in a household where my parents came from different regions – a wheat-growing area and a rice-growing one. Both had very different food preferences, as regional food varies, and we often had two styles of cuisines on the table at home to satisfy both sides! My father, who grew up in a semi-arid, land-locked region, would always want to eat dishes with less gravy to prevent the roti from becoming soggy, and never ate any fish. My mother, however, adored fish as she grew up in a region with plenty of it, freshly available. That I got to experience both styles of eating while growing up helped widen the breadth of recipes I have now at my fingertips.

In this book you will find quintessentially Bengali recipes, such as *bhortas* and *chorchoris*, Afghan recipes, such as the *chapli kabab*, Mughlai *kormas*, which have their origins in Persia, *koftas* influenced by the Turks, and even a recipe for leg of lamb whose origins can be traced back to Alexander the Great. Indian cuisine has been influenced by a myriad of culinary styles over the centuries and this has given the cuisine the depth it has in flavour and spicing.

Opposite, top: Me and Ammu celebrating Eid in Bangalore in 2013.

Opposite, bottom: A rare childhood picture of my mother on her own. Most photographs I have seen of Ammu as a child have her siblings or other relatives in the picture. She was the third daughter and was fortunate to have received a lot of time and affection from her paternal grandmother, her great grandmother, and her aunt, Shaukat Chachi, the latter of whom taught Ammu how to knit, embroider and also to cook.

## MONSOONS & MEMORIES

It rains a lot in England, but it never feels like the monsoon rains of my childhood. Usually, the monsoons arrived in the Indian month of *Sawan*. In Calcutta (now Kolkata), it felt as if it was raining continuously from the end of July. I remember watching the relentless monsoon downpour sitting on the windowsill. It was like watching an immersive theatrical performance with sounds, sights and smells: the aroma of the fragrant damp earth, the musical call of the koyal, the Indian cuckoo, as it took shelter under the leaves, and the sound of the raindrops as they fell on the stone benches in the garden. My father would pass by the window where I was sitting, humming *Megh Malhar* under his breath – a raga inspired by the monsoons. He would then break into song. One of the songs he would sing was a song of lament written by the great Sufi writer Amir Khusrau. The words are etched into my heart: '...*amma mere babul ko bhejo ri ke savan aaya savan aaya...*'. In the song, a married daughter who is no longer living near her parents is pleading with her mother to send her father to bring her home as the monsoons have arrived. Thirty monsoons have passed since I left home.

This cookbook is a collection of memories of monsoons and family meals and is dedicated to Ammu, who nurtured and nourished me. We have a bond that is hard to describe. In her, I see myself. I know she sees herself in me. Both of us are middle children – our births uncelebrated. Ammu was the third of five daughters. I was the second daughter. My mother never talks about her childhood experiences, but in the way she treated my sister Amna and me equally to my brother Arif, she showed us how every child should be cherished and treated the same. The pressure of a patriarchal society and the feeling that she let the family down by not producing a male heir when I was born was a fleeting thing for my mother. She never let that initial disappointment impact our relationship.

Above: Ammu with her siblings. From left to right standing:
Afsana, who was next oldest to my mother, Farhat who was
the next youngest, and Ammu. From left to right seated:
Rehana, the oldest and Almas, the youngest sister.

## MY JEWELLERY BOX

I was given this jewellery box when I left home as a bride. I always remember the box being called a *sunduq*, an Arabic word for box or crate. The velvet lining was changed when it was given to me, but the age of the box is evident from the stained mirror and the dents and marks along its edges. The new blue velvet covering and a deep oil varnish could not hide its age. Ammu has a similar box in India, which is larger than mine, in which she keeps her glass bangles. On the last night of every visit back home, my mother has a standard ritual: she picks a selection of her glass bangles from the box and gives them to me. I carry them carefully to England and I store them in my *sunduq*. I have rarely seen my mother not wearing bangles. If I admired the bangles she was wearing, she would almost always take them off her wrists and make me wear them. There is something deeply spiritual in this gesture. Whenever I miss Ammu, I wear one of her bangles. It comforts me to know that at one point it was hers, it has touched her hands.

When I got married, my mother gave me some of her wedding jewellery. Just as she had given my sister some when she got married. In 2017, when I opened my first restaurant in Soho, London, Ammu gave me her bridal *tika*, a headpiece with great symbolic significance. Together with her emotional side, my mother has a very down-to-earth and practical side, so she strung the headpiece into a strand so I could wear it like a locket. She pointed out that the occasions to wear a *tika* were too few and far between and that, if I got a chance, I should wear my own bridal one before I have to give it away to a future daughter-in-law!

I look at the box filled with memories. It is filled with jewellery that I remember my grandmother, my mother and my sister wearing. There are bangles in Ammu's favourite colours. There are stories linked to each piece – stories that make me laugh and cry. When my time comes, and I hand over these pieces to someone else, I will need to tell the stories of the people who wore that jewellery. Just like me, whoever gets this box is simply a custodian. The stories will need to be passed on as oral history.

In some ways, this cookbook is like my jewellery box. As a bride, these were the gifts from my family as I left home. I really discovered their value over time – not their financial worth but their emotional value. The links to family, to my heritage and to storytelling. To Ammu. These chapters tell the culinary journey of my life. Just like the box,

which is filled with layers of memories, ready to be handed over to the next generation, this book is also layered with recollections. I wrote these recipes to open my heart and share my stories with you. I hope that as you go through this book you can also return to your own food memories.

**MY RECIPE NOTEBOOK**

The pattern on the cover of this book is a depiction of *Nokshi Kantha* embroidery. These patterns are made by a simple running stitch and the technique was popular in Bengali households, but slowly fell into disuse from the 1960s as society got access to cheap clothes and fabric. The stitches would bind together discarded fabric and old sarees to strengthen them and make something useful of them once again. The small motifs cover the stains and tears in the fabric. The symbolism of the renewal and rebirth of something discarded and dismissed is especially poignant for me. This technique brings to life something that is seen as having no value by others. The uncelebrated. The fabric is given a new life and is often used to make blankets for babies or covers for pillows. The careful stitching by a woman (as it is almost always a woman) is a kind of rebirth, a celebration of resilience by using creativity and hope to cut through the darkness.

There has been a revival of this style of embroidery on both sides of the border, in West Bengal in India and in Bangladesh. Among the many similarities shared by East and West Bengalis, *Nokshi Kantha* is an important part of the shared history of the region. I have family on both sides of Bengal, so I love that the cover of my book celebrates that unity. These threads and patterns take me back to my roots.

The inspiration of using this design came from an old notebook of mine that was covered by a *Nokshi Kantha* embroidered cloth. This was the book I brought with me when I left my home in India as a new bride and moved to Cambridge. In it I wrote the postal address of all my cousins, the birthdays of my extended family, prayers for protection, some of my poems, and – importantly – some recipes. The recipes were often just random notes, annotated with diagrams to help me cook, that I had taken down while watching Ammu, my nanny, Ma, and the family cook, Haji Saheb, while they cooked. I had no idea what was important to write down as I did not know how to cook. Now I do. I've included a number of recipes in this cookbook from that notebook of 30 years ago.

## HOW TO USE THIS BOOK

This book covers a lifetime of cooking. In the first chapter, I share the comfort food of my childhood, memories of Calcutta monsoons, of understanding how food was really a language of love and how Ammu communicated by cooking and feeding. Ammu rarely expressed any emotions in words. When I left home, just like Ammu, I also used food to express my emotions. The recipes in this chapter are simple and comforting, unfussy family favourites – what I call rainy-day dishes.

The recipes in chapter two cover my early cooking days in Cambridge. After settling in England, I was cooking to ease the emptiness and hollowness I felt being away from Ammu. Uprooted from all my loved ones, food became my way home. Immersed in memories of home and the food my mother cooked, I slowly learned to cook the foods I craved. These recipes are the ones that I consider my basics, the recipes that will help you to become a more confident Indian cook.

In chapter three, I share the nostalgic dishes that I could finally create when my skills had improved. I was no longer cooking just to feed myself but also to feed others. I was transforming into Ammu – the nourisher. When I could finally recreate all the dishes I craved, my cooking moved to the next level. Lots of these dishes feed a crowd and may take a little longer than usual. These dishes are the ones you make to while away the time, for sharing with family and friends. They can be made in generous quantities and many keep well.

In chapter four, I present the recipes of celebrations – the traditional dishes cooked in my home when friends and family gathered around the table. By cooking and sharing these celebratory dishes with friends, and later my supper-club guests, I eased the pain of being away from family and missing out on the large feasts to celebrate birthdays and marriages. These recipes look stunning on the plate and are for the special occasions in your life.

The final chapter charts my journey to becoming Ammu – as a mother, I found ways to connect to my adopted home through my sons, who were both born in London. These recipes are rooted in my family traditions, but are simpler and faster to make. I know my sons will also need to make their own journeys of discovery. Identity and food are closely entwined.

Outside my London flat in Kensington, 1992. This was the first time Ammu had come to see me after I got married. I was living in Cambridge at the time, but moved to London to stay with my parents.

These recipes I make for them have all the flavours of my culinary heritage, but use more of the local produce and ingredients of my new home.

There is something universal about food memories – they linger somewhere hidden in your soul. Just as the sound of raindrops, the lyrics of a song, or the feel of a fabric can transport you to another world, so with food. The memories flood back. They take you home.

I am lucky to have Ammu to hold my hand and guide me through life, and I hope this book inspires you to cook for the Ammu in your own life, whoever they may be.

Asma

## WHAT TO COOK – SUGGESTED MENUS

I hope you will find this guide helpful. I know it can be confusing trying to decide what to cook and what goes well with what dish. You don't have to cook everything in each menu and can pick and choose depending on the time you have. A simple meal can be made out of one or two dishes listed here. The best kind of meal is the one where you can enjoy the food with friends and family. Cooking should not be exhausting, so a bit of planning before you start cooking can make it much easier. Here I have suggested things you can cook together, which work well for timing and also take into consideration the practicalities of kitchen space and utensils in a modern kitchen.

The most precious ingredient you are putting into a dish is your time. You can buy all the ingredients again, but that moment you spent cooking is a precious gift to those who will share that meal with you. Ammu would always tell me that the greatest attributes of a good cook are generosity and patience. Generosity not in buying expensive ingredients but in cooking with your heart. Patience is something that is never emphasised enough when it comes to cooking. This is not to be confused with a long, hard slog. Patience is waiting for things to marinate, for the dough to rest, to gently wash the rice... just giving each step the time it needs.

Also, never be afraid to experiment. Once you start to cook from one of my recipes, it is no longer *my* recipe – it is *yours*. You are bringing to that recipe a part of you, your unique touch, your little twists and touches to accentuate something you want to highlight in that dish. Have fun.

## WEEKNIGHT SUPPER

**Starter:**

Buttermilk Chicken Pakoras (page 244)

**Main:**

Keema Mattar (Minced Beef with Peas, page 256)

Baghare Aloo (Potatoes with Dried Red Chillies, page 104)

Saag ka Raita (Spinach with Spiced Yoghurt, page 50)

*served with rice*

## VEGAN MEAL

**Starter:**

Pyaz ke Pakora (Onion Fritters, page 30) *with* Lal Chutney (Red Chutney, page 34)

**Main:**

Saag Baadam (Spinach with Roasted Almonds, page 270)

Aloo Mattar Sabzi (Potatoes with Peas, page 46)

Bhuna Khichuri (Bengali Roasted Moong Dal and Rice, pages 134–6)

Kala Channa (Black Chickpeas, page 160)

Tomato Bhorta (Spicy Mashed Tomatoes, page 217)

**Dessert:**

Meethi Boondi (Sweet Drops in Syrup, page 68)

## VEGETARIAN/GLUTEN-FREE MEAL

**Starter:**

Aloo Bonde (Spiced Potato Balls, page 32) *with* Dhania Pudina Chutney (Coriander and Mint Chutney, page 35)

**Main:**

Aloo Gobi Mattar (Potatoes, Cauliflower and Peas, pages 94–5)

Navratan Korma (Nine-Jewel Korma, page 210)

Channa Pulao (Chickpea Pulao, page 272)

Apple, Chilli and Walnut Chutney (page 102)

**Dessert:**

Coconut Ladoo (page 70)

## PESCATARIAN MEAL

**Starter:**

Masala Fish Fry (Spicy Marinated Fish Fillets, page 80)

**Main:**

Karai Baingan (Stir-fried Aubergines, page 100)

Machher Korma (Fish Korma, page 52)

Sada Pulao (Cashew Nut and Raisin Bengali Pulao, page 198)

Lobia (Black-eyed Bean Salad, page 266)

**Dessert:**

Malpua (Ghee-fried Pancakes Soaked in Syrup, page 116)

## BRUNCH

Chingri Chop (Prawn Croquettes, page 108)

Khageena (Spicy Scrambled Eggs, page 40)

Chhita Roti (Lacy Rice Flour Roti, page 222)

Hasher Mangsho Bhuna (Spicy Duck Curry, page 220)

Saag Channa Masala (Spinach with Chickpeas, page 154)

## TOO MANY EGGS IN THE HOUSE

**Starter:**

Mini Lamb Koftas with Mint Yoghurt Dip (pages 78–9)

**Main:**

Eggs with Spiced Tomato Gravy (page 250)
*or*
Khatteh Ande (Eggs in Tamarind Gravy, page 42)

Til Wale Aloo (Spicy Sesame Potatoes, page 58)

Chapati (Wholemeal Bread, page 82)

**Dessert:**

Badam Barfi (Almond Fudge, page 166)

## BBQ WITH MEAT

**Main:**

Murgh Seekh Kabab (Chicken Seekh Kabab, page 36)

Chapli Kabab (Kabab from the North-West Frontier, page 190)

Khamiri Roti (Mughlai Roti, page 162)

Anaras Jhal Chutney (Pineapple and Chilli Chutney, page 228)

Khaas Aloo (Special Potatoes, page 208)

**Dessert:**

Zarda (Sweet Rice with Saffron and Nuts, page 168)

## DAIRY-FREE WITH MEAT

**Starter:**

Macchi Kabab (Fish Kabab, page 38)

**Main:**

Shami Kabab (Stuffed Meat Patties, page 110)

Mattar Paratha (Paratha Stuffed with Peas, page 96)

Saag Channa Masala (Spinach with Chickpeas, page 154)

Lahsun Mirch Chutney (Garlic and Chilli Chutney, page 156)

**Dessert:**

Coconut Ladoo (page 70)

## FEAST OF VEGETABLES

Baingan Pakora (Aubergine Fritters, page 88)

Baghare Aloo (Potatoes with Dried Red Chillies, page 104)

Adrak Phulli (French Beans with Ginger, page 274)

Gobi Masala (Spiced Cauliflower, page 144)

Tomato Bhorta (Spicy Mashed Tomatoes, page 217)

Saag ka Raita (Spinach with Spiced Yoghurt, page 50)

Dosti Roti (Friendship Bread, page 60)

## DATE NIGHT

**Starter:**

Buttermilk Chicken Pakoras (page 244) *with* Lal Chutney (Red Chutney, page 34)

**Soup:**

Kaddu Nariyal Shorba (Pumpkin Coconut Soup, page 48)

**Main:**

Hara Korma (Lamb Shanks in Yoghurt and Herb Gravy, page 138)

Rose, Apricot and Pistachio Pulao (page 212)

**Dessert:**

Malpua (Ghee-fried Pancakes Soaked in Syrup, page 116)

## COOKING FOR YOUR FUTURE IN-LAWS

**Starter:**

Lamb Seekh Kabab (page 242)

**Main:**

Zaffran Rogni Roti (Saffron-infused Bread, page 224)

Prawn Biryani (page 146)

Anaras Jhal Chutney (Pineapple and Chilli Chutney, page 228)

Shahi Gobi Saalan (Cauliflower in a Rich Coconut Gravy, page 188)

Safed Murgh ka Saalan (Chicken in White Gravy, page 192)

**Dessert:**

Kesar Pista Firni (Saffron and Pistachio Rice Dessert, page 230)

## FAMILY CELEBRATION

**Starter:**

Chapli Kabab (Kabab from the North-West Frontier, page 190)

Dhania Pudina Chutney (Coriander and Mint Chutney, page 35)

**Main:**

Ammu's Chicken Biryani (page 124)

Saag ka Raita (Spinach with Spiced Yoghurt, page 50)

**Dessert:**

Malpua (Ghee-fried Pancakes Soaked in Syrup, page 116) *served with* Rabri (Milk Dessert with Pistachio, page 174)

## BENGALI COMFORT FOOD

**Starter:**

Baingan Pakora (Aubergine Fritters, page 88)

**Main:**

Palong Shak Chingri (Bengali-style Prawns with Spinach, page 86)

Machher Dopiyaza (Fish with Double Onions, page 200)

Bhuna Niramish (Shredded Cabbage with Peanuts, page 254)

*served with boiled rice*

**Dessert:**

Lavender Sandesh (page 170)

## MONSOON (RAINY-DAY FOOD)

**Starter:**

Pyaz ke Pakora (Onion Fritters, page 30)

Aloo Bonde (Spiced Potato Balls, page 32)

Lal Chutney (Red Chutney, page 34)

Dhania Pudina Chutney (Coriander and Mint Chutney, page 35)

**Main:**

Khatteh Ande (Eggs in Tamarind Gravy, page 42)

Machher Mamlet (Fish Omelette, page 92)

Sabit Masoor Dal (Brown Lentils, page 90)

## INDULGENT FEAST

Golda Chingri Malaikari (Prawns Cooked in Coconut Milk, page 204)

Sikandari Raan (Spiced Leg of Lamb, pages 182–4)

Paneer Kofta (Indian Cheese Balls, page 240)

Sada Pulao (Cashew Nut and Raisin Bengali Pulao, page 198)

Zaffran Rogni Roti (Saffron-infused Bread, page 224)

**Dessert:**

Sheer Korma (Vermicelli Eid Dessert, page 232)

# Childhood

my Ammu's comfort food

**The food of my childhood** is still the food I love to eat now. Turn to this chapter when you are in need of comfort food – the dishes here are simple family favourites. There is something deeply comforting and familiar in recreating these dishes. So much has changed in my life over the decades, I could never have imagined I would live so far away from Ammu and my loved ones. In some ways, I need to cook the dishes of my childhood to capture the aromas and flavours of a time when I was free from all responsibilities. I hope they will transport you back to the past, a slower-paced time. I never realised then that those were the best days of my life.

In the first decade of my life, I lived in three different cities, as my father was transferred twice by his company. I was born in Calcutta (now called Kolkata), we then moved to Hyderabad and then to Madras (now Chennai), then back to Calcutta. I particularly remember the monsoons of Calcutta – it never rained that hard in Hyderabad or Madras. My early memories were of a calm home and mealtimes where my father would tell us stories as we ate. In this chapter, you will find rainy-day dishes, such as the *Pyaz ke Pakora* and *Aloo Bonde*, which I would eat during the monsoons; egg dishes such as *Khageena* and *Khatteh Ande*, which I remember from Hyderabad; and Bengali comfort food such as *Chingri Aloo Mattar Chorchori*. There is also a recipe for prawns that was often made for me by my nanny, Ma. It has been many years since she passed away and I thought I had come to terms with it. When I saw the hazy picture of Ma and me placed before the recipe, I was very emotional. Food can take you back to moments that you thought time had erased.

My earliest food memories are of eating with my sister on a verandah in our Calcutta flat. I must have been just under two years old. A crow flew into the verandah and stole most of the paratha we were eating. My sister Amna gave me the remaining piece that the crow had not taken. Amna and my brother Arif were both fussy eaters, but I was a very enthusiastic eater and I have a lot of memories of my siblings giving me their food to finish! Ammu would hide pieces of meat or a chop meant for Amna under the rice to make sure she did not give it to me.

Even today, Amna has that look in her eyes when she watches me eat – the way she would look at me when I ate as a child. She loved seeing me happy and one of the things that made me very happy was eating! Many years later, after I learned to cook, I cooked for my sister for the first time and I had never seen her eat with such excitement. I cooked a version of

Top left: This picture of my sister Amna and me was taken by my grandfather in Calcutta in 1972. I am the only one in the family with curly hair.

Top right: Amna and me wearing hand-knitted cardigans made by Ammu.

Bottom left: My brother Arif's first birthday in Hyderabad, 1973. The *sherwani* and *nizami* cap worn by Arif, and the *gararas*, worn by Amna and me, are traditional Muslim outfits. I disliked wearing traditional clothes as I would get entangled in them!

Bottom right: I am 7 days old in this picture, which was taken on my *aquiqa*, the traditional baby naming ceremony. The hair of the newborn baby is shaved that day and weighed and an equal weight of gold is distributed to the poor. I was very unusually given two names that day, one chosen by my great grandfather (which is the traditional way babies are named in my family) and a name my mother liked. Bapu suggested I should be called Masarat Fatima. My mother wanted to call me Asma. Bapu was always very kind to my mother and told her to call me the name she wanted. I was called Asma from then on.

Ma's Prawns (page 56) and when all the prawns in the bowl had gone, she added a spoonful of rice to mop up the remaining gravy and ate it directly from the bowl. I had a lump in my throat. During my entire childhood my sister would fuss and not eat. Yet, on a cold London evening, she was eating every morsel of food I had cooked for her with such joy. Thinking of all the food I had eaten in my childhood that was meant for Amna, that moment felt like redemption. I felt as though I was repaying her for all the food I took away from her in our childhood.

My Ammu had a deep sense of justice that I really admired. For a girl who grew up feeling the anguish of her own mother (who only had daughters) and having faced the disappointment of the family when I was born (another girl), I never remember Ammu doing anything special or extra for my brother Arif because he was a boy. The three of us were all treated equally. I look back at my childhood and try to see whether I can remember any hardships, but I only remember happy times. When we lived in Madras, once a month, Ammu would take us, my father, Ma and our family cook Islam to a restaurant. In the class-divided India of the 1970s, taking your staff to eat at the same table as you in a fancy restaurant was unusual. Ammu was gently shaking things up around her.

With grace and determination, in her late twenties with three young children and running a household on the very basic salary of my father, my mother showed a resilience and zest for life that was so admirable. I never remember her complaining. There was nothing she seemed to want. Ammu would go to the first showing of every Hindi film that was released. She loved Rajesh Khanna, the iconic Bollywood star of the 1970s. I always wondered why she would look at the film magazines from the book stall with such focus but would never buy them. Even though we always got something small from the book shop, she never bought anything – even the magazine which had Rajesh Khanna on the cover. How I wish, just once, that she had bought the glossy film magazine for herself instead of crayons for the three of us. She made it look so effortless. We never realised she was sacrificing so much for us.

Top left: With my siblings, Amna and Arif, and cousins, Sadia, Sarah and Saif, packed into an armchair in my maternal grandparent's home in Rawdon Street, Calcutta.

Top right: A rare picture with my cousins from Karachi, Pakistan. Their mother, my father's sister Phopoo Jani, was unwell and living in Cambridge for a time when I moved to England. She taught me some of the basics of cooking.

Bottom left: I wanted to dress up as a pirate for a school fancy dress competition, but Ammu convinced me to be Santa Claus. I look at the picture and I am amazed at the trouble she took to dress me up! I have no idea how she found inflatable reindeers in Hyderabad in the 1970s.

Bottom right: This was our farewell to Hyderabad in 1977. Our dear family friend, Ilyas Chachi, had ordered special children-sized garlands made with lilies and gulab (the heavily fragrant deep red Indian rose) for us. This was the first time I felt the pain of parting from a loved one.

# Pyaz ke Pakora

## Onion Fritters

My love affair with *pyaz ke pakora* goes back to the exhilaration of the first rains of the monsoons. After weeks of sweltering humidity, the relief of the cooling rain was something I still remember, even after so many decades away from India. The first rains were always a deluge. As children, we sat by the windows watching the relentless downpour, eating *pyaz ke pakora* and sipping chai. I never thought the pakoras looked like spiders until my older son visited India in monsoon season. He had just learned to speak and he looked at the pakoras and shouted 'piders'! My father has called these pakoras Piders from that day on. Serve as a snack or a starter. This goes really well with a green chutney, such as my Coriander and Mint Chutney (page 35).

### INGREDIENTS

500g onions, thinly sliced
vegetable oil, for deep-frying

*Batter*

130g gram flour (besan), sifted

⅓ tsp baking powder

2 tbsp ghee

1 tbsp fresh lemon juice

½ tsp chilli powder

¼ tsp ground turmeric

1½ tsp salt

6–8 tbsp cold water

SERVES 6–8
(2 OR 3 PAKORA PER PERSON)

METHOD

Soak the onions in cold water.

To make the batter, mix the gram flour with the baking powder and then add the ghee and mix with your hands to form crumbs. Add the lemon juice, spices and salt and gradually stir in the water to make a batter that will coat the back of a wooden spoon. Add just enough water to get the consistency of double cream.

Squeeze the onions to remove any excess moisture. Gradually add the onions to the batter to ensure the batter clings to the onions. (If you add them all at once it may make the batter too wet.)

Heat 8cm of oil in a karai or wok over a medium–high heat. Drop a tablespoon of the onion batter into the oil: the batter should spread and not become a ball. If the batter does not flatten and spread, it is too thick, so add a touch more water to it. Let the pakora cook for 1–2 minutes until crisp and golden brown, then turn and cook the other side. If your pakora browns too quickly, there is a risk it may remain raw inside. Maintain the heat of the oil at a level where the fritters take 1–2 minutes on each side and cook in batches of two or three at a time. Drain on kitchen paper as you take each batch out of the oil. Serve hot.

*Pictured with Dhania Pudina Chutney (Green Coriander and Mint Chutney, page 35).*

# Aloo Bonde

## Spiced Potato Balls in Chickpea Batter

SERVES 6 (2 OR 3 PER PERSON)

When I was growing up, you were almost guaranteed to be offered this snack if you dropped into someone's house unexpectedly. Things are very different today from the India of the 1970s and '80s. Everyone shopped from the local bazaar and there was a daily *sabzi wallah* (vegetable vendor) who carried fresh vegetables on a wooden cart and sold them outside your house. With small fridges and long hours without electricity due to power cuts, no one kept much in their refrigerators, but almost everyone had gram flour (besan) and potatoes in their kitchen, along with a trusty bottle of tomato ketchup. In today's world, it's very unlikely that you would get unexpected visitors, but if you do, this recipe is a great snack to make at short notice. Serve with a herby green or tangy red chutney (pages 35 and 34).

### INGREDIENTS

4 potatoes (about 600g in total)

1 tsp salt, plus a pinch for the cooking water

1 tbsp fresh lemon juice

¼ tsp freshly ground black pepper

1 tbsp chopped fresh coriander leaves

1 tbsp chopped fresh mint leaves

1 tsp chopped green chillies

vegetable oil, for deep-frying

*Batter*

130g gram flour (besan), sifted

⅓ tsp baking powder

2 tbsp ghee

1 tbsp fresh lemon juice

½ tsp chilli powder

¼ tsp ground turmeric

1½ tsp salt

6–8 tbsp cold water

### METHOD

Boil the potatoes in their skins with a pinch of salt until tender to the point of a knife.

Meanwhile, prepare the batter. Mix the gram flour with the baking powder, then add the ghee and mix to form crumbs. Add the lemon juice, spices and salt, then gradually stir in the water. Add just enough water to get a batter that is the consistency of double cream.

Once the potatoes are cool enough to handle, peel and mash them. Mix in the salt, lemon juice, black pepper, coriander, mint and green chillies. Shape the mixture into 2.5cm diameter balls. Dip the potato balls in the batter, ensuring they are completely coated, otherwise they will disintegrate in the hot oil.

Heat 8cm of oil in a karai or wok over a medium–high heat. Drop ½ teaspoon of the batter into the oil to test if it is ready – the batter should immediately start to sizzle and darken. If the oil is not hot enough, heat it for a bit longer and test again. Fry the *bonde* in batches of four or five at a time, turning occasionally until they are crisp and golden brown all over. Drain on kitchen paper as you take each batch out of the oil. Serve hot.

*Pictured with Lal (Red) Chutney (page 34).*

# Lal Chutney

## Red Chutney

This no-cook chutney is a spicy, tangy dipping sauce to accompany fried snacks such as Aloo Bonde (page 32) or Lamb Seekh Kabab (page 242). It can also be served as an accompaniment to a meal. The heat of the chutney is dictated by the spiciness of the chillies. I remember various versions of this chutney being made for my father when we were young. My father liked his food spicy and so there was usually a dish made for him which had a good amount of chillies in it. The Lal Chutney was made as a backup in case he found the food too mild! Any leftover chutney can be kept in a sealed container for a couple of days – but a word of warning: the heat will increase the following day as the chillies infuse further. The texture is similar to a salsa and it is worth splashing out a bit and getting really good tomatoes for this chutney.

*Pictured on pages 33 and 96.*

SERVES 8–10

INGREDIENTS

1 tsp cumin seeds

500g ripe red tomatoes, finely chopped

3–4 hot jalapeño chillies, finely chopped

3 garlic cloves, finely chopped

1 tsp fresh lime juice

¼ tsp salt

1 tbsp chopped dried apricots

2 tbsp chopped fresh coriander

1 tbsp coconut oil, sesame oil or olive oil

½ tsp honey

METHOD

Dry roast the cumin seeds in a heavy-based pan over a low heat, stirring until they turn a few shades darker. Tip them onto a plate and leave to cool.

When cool, grind the seeds to a powder, using a spice grinder or a pestle and mortar.

Mix all the other ingredients together in a bowl. Add the ground cumin seeds and mix well, then taste and adjust the seasoning. Cover the bowl and leave at room temperature for a couple of hours for the flavours to infuse before serving.

# Dhania Pudina Chutney

## Coriander and Mint Chutney

We never had a food processor in my house when I was young. This chutney was made on a *sil batta* (in Bengal it was called a *shil nora*), a stone grinder that comes in two pieces: a flat heavy piece at the bottom and an oblong stone. The bottom piece would be scarred with a chisel and hammer at regular intervals to create a rough surface. The fresh chutney ingredients were put on top of the flat stone and the oblong stone was then rolled over the fresh ingredients to crush and break them down to a paste. The aroma that rose as the mint and coriander were crushed between the stones is one of my favourite childhood aromatic memories.

Just after I moved to England, I managed to convince my husband to carry back a *sil batta* in his luggage on one of his business trips to Dhaka (he had a bigger luggage allowance). He was not impressed at having to carry a huge stone in his luggage until I made him the chutney in the traditional way. Once he had watched the process and tasted the chutney, he never again complained about the stone!

If you do get hold of a stone grinder (or even a good heavy pestle and mortar), start by pounding the ginger so that it's broken down into shreds, then set it aside. Next, pound the coriander and the mint, followed by the green chillies (broken into pieces). Add the salt and the ginger back in and continue to grind, gradually adding the remaining ingredients until they form a rough paste. Add the water in stages when grinding, as you may not need the full amount. You can use a food processor for speed if this sounds too much, but I think it tastes better when it's pounded!

*Pictured on pages 31 and 245.*

MAKES 6–8 TABLESPOONS

INGREDIENTS

1-cm piece of fresh ginger

100g fresh mint leaves, shredded

100g fresh coriander leaves and upper stems, roughly chopped

3 green chillies

2 tbsp fresh lemon juice

1 tbsp brown sugar

1 tsp salt

4 tbsp cold water

METHOD

Place all the ingredients in a food processor and blend to a smooth paste.

Alternatively, grind each ingredient separately using a pestle and mortar, then mix together in a bowl.

Serve immediately, or cover and keep in the fridge for up to 2 days.

# Murgh Seekh Kabab

## Chicken Seekh Kabab Grilled with Ginger and Pickled Shallots

SERVES 6–8

The addition of ginger and pickled onions here adds an extra layer of flavour to the chicken as it cooks. Our cook, Haji Saheb, would sit on his haunches basting the kabab, which was cooked on a tray of charcoal on the driveway outside the kitchen. He would hold a *pankha* (a traditional Bengali fan made of palm leaf with a wooden handle) and fan the embers while turning the *seekhs* (skewers) to ensure even cooking. I always associate this kabab with the swishing noise of the fan – and my mother asking me not to stand so close to the grill. I loved seeing the sparks flying out as the ghee dripped down into the charcoal.

The kabab can be grilled indoors or cooked on a barbecue. Serve with *Lobia* (page 266) for a summer barbecue or with *Zaffran Rogni Roti* (page 224) in colder months.

### INGREDIENTS

900g boneless, skinless chicken thighs, cut into 2.5-cm cubes

5-cm piece of fresh ginger, thinly sliced

300g well-drained pickled shallots or onions (home-made or from a jar)

6 tbsp ghee or vegetable oil

*Marinade*

juice of 2 lemons

¾ tsp sugar

2 garlic cloves, crushed

3-cm piece of fresh ginger, grated

1 tsp chilli powder

### METHOD

Combine all the marinade ingredients in a bowl. Add the chicken, turning it to coat all of it in the marinade. Cover and transfer to the fridge to marinate, ideally for 4 hours. If you're really short of time, even 30 minutes marinating can make a difference.

Preheat the grill to high.

Thread the chicken onto 6–8 skewers, alternating the chicken pieces with the ginger slices and pickled onions. Grill for about 5 minutes on each side, basting the meat with the ghee or oil so it cooks evenly.

Serve hot.

# Macchi Kabab

## Fish Kabab

I have so many memories of eating this kabab as a child, with *Bhuna Khichuri* (page 134) or with plain rice and dal. There were two versions: one for important guests and visitors, and a simpler one for the family. I only discovered later that it was only the shape and the way it was cooked that differed – the mixture was the same!

Crab can be substituted for the fish. One of my cousins adapted this recipe in his first year at university, when he was very homesick – he used tinned tuna, which he could buy in the local shop! Inspired by his story, I made this fish kabab with tinned salmon (removing the skin and bones) and it worked. If you do make this with tinned fish, you need to drain it very well and the seasoning may need to be adjusted.

### INGREDIENTS

800g–1kg firm white fish fillet

¼ tsp ground turmeric

1 tsp freshly ground black pepper

½ tsp salt

1 tbsp fresh lemon juice

2 slices of white bread, crusts removed

60g red onion, finely chopped

1 small garlic clove, crushed (or ½ tsp garlic paste)

5-mm piece of fresh ginger, grated (or ½ tsp ginger paste)

2 tbsp finely chopped fresh coriander leaves

½–1 tsp chopped fresh chilli (avoid the super-hot varieties, such as Scotch bonnet or bird's eye)

SERVES 6–8

1 egg, beaten

melted butter or vegetable oil, for cooking

### To Serve

sea salt, lemon wedges, fresh green chillies, and red onions, sliced into rings

### METHOD

Steam the fish until cooked through. Remove any skin or bones, then flake the pieces into a bowl and mix with the turmeric, pepper, salt and lemon juice. Leave to stand for 15 minutes.

Meanwhile, soak the bread in cold water then squeeze out all the liquid and crumble the bread into little lumps. Mix the bread into the fish mixture, ensuring it is evenly distributed. Add the chopped onion, garlic, ginger, coriander, chilli and egg and gently knead to form a paste. Leave to rest for 10 minutes.

There are two ways to complete this kabab: For the home-style version, use damp hands to divide the mixture into 24 even-sized balls, then flatten each one into a patty, 5cm in diameter and 1.5cm thick. Heat a little oil in a frying pan over a medium heat and shallow-fry the patties in batches for just over 1 minute on each side until golden. Drain on kitchen paper.

The guest version is grilled on skewers so it looks a bit more fancy. Preheat the grill to medium, or cook on a low–medium barbecue. Use damp hands to press 2 tablespoons of the mixture onto each skewer to form a sausage, 10cm long and about 2cm thick. Grill, turning the kababs frequently and basting with melted butter or oil, for 3–4 minutes until golden.

Serve with a sprinkling of sea salt, lemon wedges, green chillies and sliced red onions.

# Khagheena

## Spicy Scrambled Eggs

SERVES 4

This was the standard breakfast when the family gathered for a celebration or wedding, because it was so simple to make for lots of people. *Khageena* was often served with a side platter of chapatis (page 82), which were generously layered with ghee and rolled up.

I realised much later why our cooks made these eggs for breakfast on these occasions – to get breakfast out of the way so they could focus on cooking for the main event or dinner that night. Cooking a large dish of eggs meant they did not have to make individual breakfasts for the family as they woke up.

The cooks would use the best eggs for this. In my parents' ancestral homes, they always kept chickens and so would get fresh eggs – they were called *desi anda* (local eggs). In the city, most of the eggs we got were from farms, but for family celebrations and weddings that took place in the city, the cooks would make a special effort and get *desi anda*, to make sure the relatives visiting from the ancestral homes did not comment on the poor quality of food we ate in the city!

INGREDIENTS

2 tbsp vegetable oil

2 large white onions, chopped

3 large tomatoes, chopped

3 green chillies, chopped

8 large eggs

1 tsp ground turmeric

½ tsp chilli powder

½ tsp salt

chopped fresh coriander, to garnish

METHOD

Heat the oil over a medium–high heat and fry the onions until they soften. Add the tomatoes and chillies and cook until softened.

Meanwhile, beat the eggs in a bowl.

Add the turmeric and chilli powder to the onion and tomato mix, stir for 30 seconds and then pour in the beaten eggs. Reduce the heat to medium–low. Keep stirring until the eggs are softly set. Add the salt, then taste and check the seasoning as you may need to add more.

Garnish with coriander and serve warm.

# Khatteh Ande

## Eggs in Tamarind Gravy

Eggs are monsoon food! When the rainy season began in Calcutta, we waited for the days of relentless rain, because what came after that was waterlogged streets. No school. No electricity for days as the power stations were under water. Food rationing because the bazaars were closed. But eggs were delivered to us by the *anda wallah* (the egg man), who would cycle through streets that were knee-deep in water and bring us 24 eggs every other day. At first, everyone got a whole egg, but if the rains continued, we would get only half an egg a day. The eggs were always prepared with great care and mealtimes were something of an occasion, with a lantern at the edge of the table, followed by a long night of storytelling by my father.

### INGREDIENTS

6–8 large hard-boiled eggs

6 tbsp vegetable oil

2 onions, cut in half and thinly sliced

1 large garlic clove, crushed
(or ¾ tsp garlic paste)

2-cm piece of fresh ginger, grated
(or 1 tsp ginger paste)

¾ tsp ground turmeric

½ tsp chilli powder

3 tbsp tamarind extract

400ml water

pinch of salt

50g fresh coriander, chopped, plus a handful
to garnish

pinch of sugar (optional)

### METHOD

Shell the hard-boiled eggs and make three shallow slits on the surface of each one. This will help the eggs absorb the tamarind gravy. Set aside.

Heat the oil in a deep pan over a medium–high heat. Add the onions and stir until they start to lightly caramelise. Add the garlic and ginger, then the turmeric and chilli powder, and continue to cook, stirring frequently, for a further 4–5 minutes until the raw smell of the garlic and ginger has gone. Add the tamarind extract, water and a good pinch of salt, then reduce the heat to a simmer. Add the chopped coriander and simmer until the liquid has reduced by half.

Add the hard-boiled eggs and cook, uncovered, over a low heat for 10 minutes. If you would like the dish to have a sweet and sour taste, you can add a good pinch of sugar at this point.

Garnish with extra coriander and serve warm.

Above and right: Chhatari Fortress, the ancestral home of my father. The hallway or *diwan*, above, was where disputes over land and taxes were decided by my ancestors. It was also a place for royal receptions and formal events. The women in the family had their own passage and screened windows on a raised floor so they could watch the proceedings in the hall. The archway leads into the *haveli*, where the women lived. The windows grilles were made of carved marble. This allowed the air to circulate in the *haveli*, but screened the women from strangers. Sadly, the original kitchens adjoining the building fell into ruin and nothing remains of them today. It is said that the kitchens were always guarded so that no one could poison the food that was served to the family. Feasts are now prepared in the courtyard (see opposite). Whenever we have a big feast, there are running battles with monkeys who turn up in large numbers and try to steal food. I remember my sons' amazement a few years ago when the gang of monkeys descended into the courtyard in a coordinated attack. One of the monkeys turned on the hosepipe and started spraying all the cooks and managed to put out most of the fires. In the confusion, the other monkeys stole a lot of the food and took it to the roof to eat.

Right: Bano grilling kababs over coals in the courtyard of my parent's home. Bano assisted Haji Saheb over the years and learned to prepare all the family dishes. Unlike the palm leaf fan Haji Saheb used, Bano would use a thin piece of wood to fan and control the fire.

Below: A *daawat*, a family feast, also being prepared in the courtyard. The practicalities of cooking for a large number of people requires the food to be cooked outdoors over fire, to grill meats and prepare rotis.

Bottom: Outside the kitchen of Lazeez Catering. I am standing next to Ma, behind me is Islam, and in the shadows is Haji Saheb – a tall, graceful man who dedicated his life to looking after us. From left to right are Dhamal, Verma, Rani, Salma, and the *sabzi wallah*, the vegetable vendor who would return to our kitchen for chai and a chat after he had finished his rounds.

# Aloo Mattar Sabzi

## Potatoes with Peas

SERVES 4–6

Once a year, we would make the long train journey from Calcutta to Aligarh to visit my father's family. The trip could take two nights and a day. Going by train was the most convenient way to travel as there was no airport in the town. We were allowed to eat this dish at the station while we waited for our train, as my mother could see it being made in front of us and it was steaming hot. It was served with *kachuri*, round fried bread. On the journey, we would cross mighty rivers and pass endless villages and farmlands along the way. As we moved out of Bengal, my father would buy us 'safe' food from the stations we stopped at. Usually it was variations on potatoes and *puris*. Occasionally, we got a treat of ice cream followed by chai. I always associate this dish with the journey I used to make with my family. I never realised then how precious those moments were. It is so unlikely we will ever make that journey again – just the five of us.

This is a good recipe to spice up a meal with minimum effort. It can be eaten with grilled fish, roast meat or even an omelette. If you have any leftovers, stuff the potatoes and peas into a toastie – it tastes delicious! You need to use standard white potatoes, not new potatoes and not floury or baking potatoes, which would break up too much. Eat it with Chapati (page 82) or Dosti Roti (page 60), with a chutney, such as Apple, Chilli and Walnut (page 102).

### INGREDIENTS

1 tbsp vegetable oil

½ tsp cumin seeds

5 whole dried red chillies

500g white potatoes, boiled in their skins

1 tsp ground turmeric

200g frozen peas

1 tsp salt, or to taste

500ml warm water

Indian flatbreads (any kind), to serve

### METHOD

Heat the oil in a pan over a high heat. Add the cumin seeds and chillies, then immediately reduce the heat, as you do not want the spice and chillies to burn.

Roughly break the potatoes into lumps (I keep the skins on) and add to the pan. Add the turmeric and stir the potatoes and spices for a couple of minutes. Add the frozen peas and salt, followed by the warm water.

Cook the potatoes over a high heat for a further 5 minutes until there is a glossy shine on the potatoes. The texture should not be dry. Taste and adjust the seasoning before serving.

This is a thick dish that's meant to be scooped up and eaten with any kind of Indian bread.

# Kaddu Nariyal Shorba

## Pumpkin Coconut Soup

SERVES 6

Nothing had prepared me for the damp, cold winters of Cambridge. I wanted to make this soup not just because it was warming and comforting, but because I also got a lot of free pumpkins from the market on my first Hallowe'en in England. I was surprised to see the number of pumpkins on sale. The shop owner gave me a free one to take home as he was amused that I did not know anything about Hallowe'en! After that, I would buy a pumpkin from him whenever I saw him. I made a lot of pumpkin soup in the first autumn after I moved to England.

In Bengal, the most prized pumpkin is a variety with sweet, deep-orange flesh, and this soup does taste best when made with a sweeter variety of pumpkin. The combination of pumpkin and coconut works beautifully here with the flavours of fennel seeds and dried red chillies.

### INGREDIENTS

2 tbsp vegetable oil

3 dried red chillies, broken

2 heaped tbsp fennel seeds

1 star anise

20g white onion, chopped

4-cm piece of fresh ginger, grated

6 large garlic cloves, crushed

750g pumpkin (preferably an orange-fleshed variety), peeled and chopped into chunks

1 tsp salt

200ml thick coconut milk (tinned)

sugar, to taste

coconut cream, to garnish

### METHOD

Warm the oil in a large pan over a medium–high heat. In quick succession, add the broken dried chillies, fennel seeds and star anise, followed by the onion, ginger and garlic, then cook, stirring, for a few minutes. Stir in the pumpkin and add enough warm water to cover, along with the salt. Bring to the boil, then reduce the heat, cover and simmer for 15–20 minutes until the pumpkin is tender.

Use a hand blender to whizz the contents of the pan until smooth.

Put the pan back over a low heat to warm through. Stir in the coconut milk, then taste for seasoning, adding sugar and salt to suit your taste.

Serve in bowls, with some coconut cream swirled on top of the soup.

# Saag ka Raita

## Spinach with Spiced Yoghurt

SERVES 8–10

Until I left India in 1991, I had not eaten any vegetable that was out of season. This was not because my family was trying to eat seasonally, support local farmers or be sustainable. In the 1970s and '80s in India, it was simply how every family ate. There were very few air-conditioned supermarkets selling fresh produce and we did not have refrigerated lorries transporting perishable goods between the regional states. Everyone purchased their vegetables in the local bazaar or from their local street vendor. Spinach was a winter speciality and I looked forward to the first sight of spinach in the bazaar. My mother would wait until the middle of the spinach season to buy it, as the leaves were bigger and the flavour stronger. We would usually add it to meat or potatoes. When there was a glut of spinach and the price fell, we would add spinach to the raita. I always associate this raita with winter school holidays.

This is a great recipe for using up the half bag of spinach left in your fridge! The marbled white and green colours of the raita look lovely and it has a nice texture, too. This raita goes well with meat or vegetables, but ideally serve it with food that does not have a lot of gravy, so it does not get diluted with the gravy when served on a plate. It goes particularly well with Pot-Roast Beef (page 150) or with Keema Mattar (Minced Beef with Peas, page 256).

### INGREDIENTS

500g fresh spinach leaves

½ tsp cumin seeds

1kg full-fat Greek-style yoghurt

1 tsp salt, or to taste

¼ tsp chilli powder

2 tbsp pomegranate seeds

### METHOD

Place the spinach in a colander over a pan of boiling water and steam until tender. Spread the leaves on a deep plate and cut into strips – reserve the liquid that is released. Leave to cool.

Dry roast the cumin seeds in a heavy-based pan over a low heat, stirring until they turn a few shades darker. Tip them onto a plate and leave to cool.

When cool, grind to a powder, using a spice grinder or a pestle and mortar.

Whisk the yoghurt in a bowl until it is smooth. Stir in the cooled spinach and its liquid, followed by the salt, chilli powder and ground cumin seeds. Taste and adjust the seasoning.

Sprinkle the pomegranate seeds over the top before serving.

# Machher Korma

## Fish Korma

There is a difference between Bengali cuisine and Bengali Mughlai cuisine. Traditional Bengali food cooked at home is most commonly boiled rice, fresh local fish (often cooked with turmeric in mustard oil), seasonal vegetables cooked with *panch phoran* or mustard seeds, side dishes of *bhajja* (fried vegetables), such as aubergines, and always something *tok* or sour – and the grand finale... *mishti* (dessert). Bengali Mughlai food, on the other hand, is more meat-based, with longer, slower cooking. The dishes are heavily influenced by the food traditions of Delhi and Lucknow, and do not use a lot of turmeric or cumin. This fish korma is an interesting dish, in which the two cooking traditions come together. I loved fish korma because it was milder than the usual fish curries and I did not have a very high tolerance for chillies when I was young. Traditionally, this would be made with *rui*, a local carp. If you are adept at deboning fish, by all means use a fish that is more local to you, but for ease of eating I have suggested boneless fish fillet.

This is a good weeknight meal as it doesn't take long for the fish to cook. Serve with boiled rice or flatbreads to mop up the juices. It also keeps well if you are not feeding a large group – store in the fridge for up to two days.

SERVES 8–10

### INGREDIENTS

1.5kg skinless, boneless fish fillets, such as cod or halibut

3 tsp salt

generous pinch of saffron strands

2 tbsp full-fat milk

100ml ghee

2 tbsp vegetable oil

1 large white onion, thinly sliced into half moons

2 bay leaves

5-cm piece of cinnamon stick

4 green cardamom pods

1 tbsp crushed garlic (or garlic paste)

2 tbsp crushed fresh ginger (or ginger paste)

1 tsp medium chilli powder

250ml full-fat Greek-style yoghurt

600ml warm water

1 tsp sugar

1 tbsp raisins (optional)

slivered almonds, to garnish

### METHOD

Cut the fish into 8–10 equal portions. Rub 1 teaspoon of the salt over all sides of the fish and set aside for 30 minutes.

Put the saffron in a small bowl. Warm the milk to tepid and pour it over the saffron, then set aside.

*Continues overleaf*

In a wide, shallow pan, heat the ghee and oil over a medium–high heat. Add the onion and fry for about 15 minutes until caramelised. Using a slotted spoon, remove the onion from the pan, leaving as much oil in the pan as possible, and spread the onion on a plate so it crisps as it cools.

Add the fish to the pan and quickly fry until it just begins to turn opaque – do not let the fillets cook through. You may need to fry the fish in batches. As soon as it's done, remove and place on a tray, leaving as much of the oil in the pan as possible. Turn off the heat when you are frying the last batch of fish.

Grind the caramelised onion to a paste, using a blender or a pestle and mortar.

Put the pan back over a medium–high heat and add the bay leaves, cinnamon and cardamoms. Stir for a few seconds and then add the garlic and ginger and cook, stirring, for a minute. If they are burning or sticking to the base of the pan, add a splash of water. Add the remaining salt, the onion paste, chilli powder, yoghurt and warm water. Reduce the heat to medium and bring to the boil, then simmer for about 10 minutes until the liquid has reduced slightly and you can see the oil coming to the surface.

Gently return the fish fillets to the pan and cover with the gravy. If possible, cook the fillets in a single layer as this will prevent them from breaking up. Reduce the heat, add the sugar and the saffron-infused milk (and raisins, if using) and cook, uncovered, until the fish is cooked – this should take no longer than 5–7 minutes. If you are using thicker fish steaks, you will need to cover the pan briefly to ensure the fish is cooked all the way through, but be careful not to overcook the fish.

Serve hot, garnished with slivered almonds.

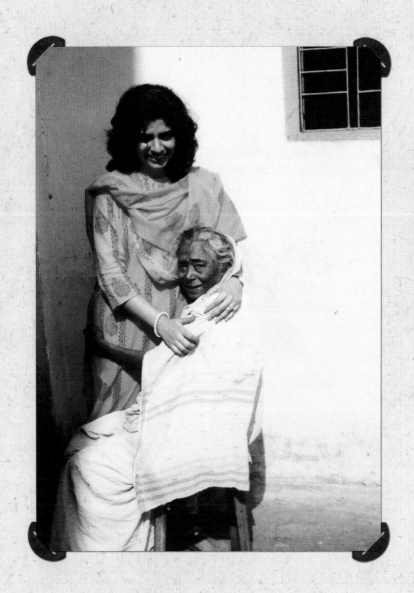

This picture was taken the night before my wedding.
I was wearing a yellow *shalwar kameez* in preparation
for my *haldi* and henna night. I kept looking for Ma, who
had been my nanny, and could not see her in the house.
Eventually, I discovered her sitting outside near
the kitchen. I realised she did not want to see the rituals
of the pre-wedding ceremony. She asked me, 'Will you
forget me when you leave?' How could I ever forget her?!

# Ma's Prawns

SERVES 6

Ma was a formidable person. She came to help my grandmother look after my mother when she was born. When my mother got married, Ma moved to my parents' flat and was an integral part of our household. We were her family. We all called her Ma, or 'mother', which may have seemed strange to outsiders, who probably saw her as a regular *ayah* or *bua* (a traditional nursemaid – having a live-in carer to look after the children was a common practice in Indian households who could afford to keep one).

When Ma died, I could not go to her funeral. In the Islamic tradition, my brother carried her down to her grave: this is usually done by a child or relative. Ma would have been pleased to have seen the send-off she got: the local bazaar was closed in her honour and the street outside our house was full of people who came to pay their respects. A lady of substance.

This is the prawn dish she always made for me whenever I returned home from England. It's a simple, heart-warming, no-fuss dish, that only takes 45 minutes or so to make. I eat Ma's Prawns with plain boiled rice.

## INGREDIENTS

3 onions

150ml mustard oil (if you can't find it, use vegetable oil)

1 tsp ginger paste

½ tsp garlic paste

½ tsp ground turmeric

1½ tsp chilli powder

½ tsp ground cumin

½ tsp ground coriander

2 green chillies, slit in half

1 tsp salt

1.25kg raw peeled prawns, deveined

fresh coriander, to garnish

**Note** If you are using mustard oil you need to heat it to smoking point to reduce the pungency of the oil. Please ensure your kitchen is well ventilated so the oil does not set off the smoke alarm. Leave the oil to cool slightly before starting the recipe.

## METHOD

Put the onions in a food processor and blitz to a paste. (Ma would have used a stone grinder, in the way described on page 35.)

Heat the oil in a heavy-based pan over a medium–high heat. Add half of the onion paste and cook until it turns light brown. Add the remaining onion paste, ginger, garlic, turmeric, chilli powder, cumin, ground coriander, green chillies, salt and 4 tablespoons of water and bring to the boil. Reduce the heat, cover and simmer for 15 minutes.

Remove the lid, increase the heat and cook the paste until you can see the oil coming to the surface. Add the prawns and cook, uncovered, over a medium heat for 10–15 minutes until the prawns have changed colour and are cooked through.

Serve immediately, garnished with coriander.

# Til Wale Aloo

## Spicy Sesame Potatoes

SERVES 4–6

These are very versatile and can be served with roast meat or salad. At home, this dish was made with small, oval potatoes that were usually left whole. They were often misshapen and I remember Jameila, one of our staff, triumphantly pouring out these small potatoes from her jute shopping bag, as she would usually get them for free from the *sabzi wallah*, the vegetable vendor in the market. The vendor would have struggled to sell such small, odd-shaped potatoes, so Jameila would get them to make staff lunch and would send a bowl for us to eat, too. I tried using early new potatoes when I moved to England and they worked beautifully. Serve this with Amla Chutney (Gooseberry Chutney, page 62) and Chapati (page 82). It also makes a good accompaniment to Eggs with Spiced Tomato Gravy (page 250) or Khatteh Ande (Eggs in Tamarind Gravy, page 42).

### INGREDIENTS

500g Jersey Royals or new potatoes

3–5 whole dried red chillies

1 tbsp vegetable oil

1 tsp sesame seeds

½ tsp ground turmeric

1 tsp salt, plus a pinch for the cooking water

### METHOD

Wash the potatoes to remove all the dirt, but leave the skins on. Depending on the size of the potatoes, leave them whole or cut them into halves or quarters, so they are all roughly the same size. Par-boil them in a pan of water and add a generous pinch of salt to the water. Do not let the potatoes cook all the way through. Drain the potatoes and spread on a plate so they cool quickly.

If you want a spicy dish, break the dried chillies in half. If you want the flavour of the chillies without the added heat, leave the chillies whole and use only three.

Once the potatoes have cooled, heat the oil in a pan over a high heat. Add the sesame seeds and dried chillies, then immediately reduce the heat, as you do not want the seeds and chillies to burn. Add the turmeric, then add the potatoes and stir for a few minutes. Add the salt. To prevent the potatoes from sticking to the pan, add a splash of water and keep stirring. The potatoes should take on a golden shade.

Taste and adjust the seasoning and check that the potatoes are cooked through before serving.

# Dosti Roti

## Friendship Bread

This is a wonderful, soft bread. Two rotis are rolled together with a layer of butter and a sprinkling of flour between them, then, when the bread is cooked, the two 'friends' separate into two individual rotis. As one side of the joined roti does not touch the hot *tawa* or griddle, the bread stays soft. This unusual cooking process gives the roti a wonderful texture. It's a classic two-for-the-price-of-one deal! Watching the cook separate the rotis was always so exciting for me.

These can be eaten with so many things and in so many different ways – make them to serve with Methi Chicken (Chicken with Fenugreek, page 152) or Dum ki Murgh (Baked Chicken, page 214). Don't be put off making your own – it is worth it and they are much less complicated to make than yeast-leavened breads.

### INGREDIENTS

450g chapati flour or wholemeal flour (weighed after sifting and discarding the bran left in the sieve), plus extra for dusting

½ tsp salt

300ml warm water

50g butter, melted

### SERVES 6 (MAKES 12 ROTIS)

### METHOD

Mix the flour and salt in a bowl. Make a well in the centre and gradually add the water – you may not need to add it all – to make a soft but pliable dough. Cover and leave to rest for 2 hours.

Divide the dough into 12 pieces and shape each piece into a ball. On a lightly floured surface, roll out each ball to a 10-cm circle. As you roll out the circles, cover them with a damp tea towel and keep them in a single layer (don't stack them).

Once you have rolled out all 12 circles, brush the top of half of them with melted butter followed by a thin dusting of flour. Stick one of the unbuttered circles on top of a buttered circle. Sprinkle with flour and gently roll out the joined bread to make a 20-cm circle. Repeat until you have six double-decker rotis.

Heat a *tawa*, griddle or frying pan over a medium–high heat. Cook one roti at a time, pressing down the edges with scrunched-up kitchen paper or a clean kitchen cloth until the bread puffs up. Turn and cook on the other side in the same way. The roti will start to separate. Take it off the *tawa* and pull the two sides apart.

Wrap the hot rotis in a cloth to keep warm while you cook the remaining rotis.

# Amla Chutney

## Fresh Gooseberry Chutney

When I was a child in India, I would often accompany my mother to New Market, the covered market in Calcutta where you could buy everything from baby clothes to sacks of onions. We usually went to buy spices and vegetables. Once we reached the vegetable section, my mother would spend a long time selecting vegetables and haggling prices. I would sit on a bench and pick fruits from the display. My mother would add an extra 5 rupees to the bill for things I may have eaten. If gooseberries were in season, I would always start with them: I loved their tart, sharp taste. Gooseberries were only briefly available in the colder months after Christmas. The gooseberry season was also the season of oranges and fresh jaggery, so sometimes fresh jaggery syrup was used to sweeten this chutney. You can replace the honey with any kind of sugar, maple syrup or agave nectar, and the orange juice with another fruit juice, such as apple, pineapple or cranberry. We would have this fresh gooseberry chutney with plain rice and Sabit Masoor Dal (Brown Lentils, page 90), or with Til Wale Aloo (Spicy Sesame Potatoes, page 58) and Chapati (page 82).

**SERVES 6**

### INGREDIENTS

250g gooseberries, washed, dried, topped and tailed

50g raisins

50g red onion, finely chopped

1 green chilli, finely chopped

3 tbsp orange juice

2 tsp honey

½ tsp freshly ground black pepper

2 tsp salt

### METHOD

Finely dice the gooseberries and set aside.

Put the raisins, onion and chilli in a bowl and mix in the orange juice, honey, black pepper and salt. Stir in the diced gooseberries, then cover and chill for at least 1 hour before serving.

This will keep in a covered container in the fridge for 5–6 days.

# Hussainy Curry

## Skewered Beef in Gravy

For years, I thought this was a Bengali dish
influenced by Muslim culinary traditions,
due to the name. I then discovered it was an
Anglo-Indian dish made in Calcutta and eastern
India during colonial times. Sadly, many Anglo-
Indian dishes are at risk of disappearing from
our culinary heritage, as the community is
now dispersed around the world. In Calcutta,
I went to La Martiniere, an Anglican school
established in 1836, and later to university
at an all-girls Roman Catholic college run by
Irish nuns. Many of the nuns would wear a
simple cotton saree instead of the usual habit
and many spoke fluent Hindi or Bengali! In
the 1980s, Calcutta was still a melting pot
of different cultures. I was fortunate to have
Anglo-Indian friends in school and college, and
got to eat some of the distinctive dishes of their
community, such as this delicious curry. I have
also eaten versions of this dish where the cook
has added thick coconut milk at the end to make
a rich sauce. I serve this with the Cashew Nut
and Raisin Bengali Pulao (page 198), or you can
make any rice recipe. You will need 16–20 thin
bamboo skewers, about 15–20 cm long.

### INGREDIENTS

250g full-fat Greek-style yoghurt

1 tsp ground turmeric

2 tsp salt

1kg beef (in India we use undercut, but here
I use rump steak), cut into 2.5-cm cubes

4 tbsp vegetable oil

2 onions, sliced into half moons

SERVES 4–6

1 tsp garlic paste

1 tbsp ginger paste

2 tsp chilli powder

500ml warm water

120ml thick coconut milk (optional)

### METHOD

In a large bowl, mix the yoghurt with ½ teaspoon
turmeric and 1½ teaspoons salt. Add the beef
cubes and leave to marinate for at least 4 hours.

Thread about 6 cubes of meat onto each skewer.
Don't pack the skewers too tightly, or the meat
will not cook all the way through.

In a heavy-based pan with a lid, heat the oil over
a medium–high heat. Add the onions and fry
until caramelised. Using a slotted spoon, remove
the onions from the pan and set aside.

Add the garlic and ginger pastes to the pan and stir
until the raw smell has gone. Add the remaining
turmeric and salt, the chilli powder and warm
water. Put the onions in a food processor and
blitz to a paste, then add to the pan. Bring the
mixture to the boil, then layer the skewers in the
pan. Bring back to a rolling boil, reduce the heat,
cover and simmer for about 45 minutes.

Check that the meat is cooked and tender. You
may need to simmer it for longer (up to 1 hour),
depending on the cut and age of the beef. When
the meat is tender, remove the lid. Taste and
add more salt if needed. Add the coconut milk,
if using, and simmer until the liquid has reduced
to a fairly thick gravy and you can see the oil
coming to the surface. Serve with rice.

# Chingri Aloo Mattar Chorchori

## Prawns with Peas and Potatoes

SERVES 4–6

A *chorchori* is a generic Bengali description of a dish in which more than a couple of vegetables are cooked in oil. There is no gravy, and the vegetables are meant to hold their shape and not disintegrate. You need to use standard white potatoes, not new potatoes and not floury or baking potatoes, which would break up too much. This is the perfect accompaniment to rice and dal dishes. If you cannot find small prawns, you can use bigger prawns cut into 1-cm pieces.

### INGREDIENTS

6 tbsp vegetable oil

½ tsp kalonji (nigella seeds)

400g white potatoes, peeled and cut into 2.5-cm cubes

2 large onions, thinly sliced into half moons

1 tsp ground turmeric

1 tsp chilli powder

1½ tsp salt

100ml water

100g shelled peas

2 green chillies, slit in half

500g raw peeled small prawns, deveined

### METHOD

Heat the oil in a *karai* or wok over a high heat. When it is hot, lower the heat to medium, add the nigella seeds and stir for a few seconds, then add the potatoes. Stir-fry for 7–8 minutes or until the potatoes start to brown at the edges.

Add the onions, turmeric, chilli powder and salt and stir-fry for a few more minutes. Add the water and cook over a medium–high heat until the liquid has reduced by half.

Add the shelled peas and green chillies and continue to cook until all the water has been absorbed. Add the prawns and stir-fry until the prawns are cooked.

Taste and adjust the seasoning before serving.

# Meethi Boondi

## Sweet Drops in Syrup

SERVES 4–6

These tiny golden drops were the most popular dessert distributed in religious celebrations. The convenience of giving a box of *meethi boondi* to any family was that there would be enough for everyone. Unlike other sweets that were larger and harder to divide, these were delightful, even if someone only got to eat a couple of spoonfuls. I make these now for festive family occasions. I have used only one colour for these drops, but in India it is common to have some in red or green. This is easy, as you just take out a bit of batter and mix in the food colouring.

To make these, you will need a skimmer with holes about 3mm in diameter – bigger or smaller holes will not work as well. It is a very thrilling process once you get confident and collect your harvest of perfectly fried tiny balls from the oil.

### INGREDIENTS

*Boondi*

120g gram flour (besan)

¼ tsp bicarbonate of soda

120ml water

50:50 ghee and vegetable oil, for deep-frying

*Sugar Syrup*

200ml water

4 green cardamom pods

2 cloves

200g caster sugar

⅛ tsp saffron strands

few drops of saffron food colouring (optional)

### METHOD

Sift the flour and bicarb together into a bowl. Gradually stir in the water to make a smooth, pancake-like batter. Set aside for 20 minutes.

Meanwhile, prepare the sugar syrup. Put the water in a pan with the cardamoms and cloves and bring to the boil. Add the sugar and stir until it has dissolved. Boil the syrup for 5 minutes at a slow rolling boil, then take the pan off the heat.

After the batter has rested, stir in a couple of tablespoons of water to loosen it. Heat 4cm of ghee and oil in a deep frying pan over a medium heat. Hold the skimmer just above the oil. Pour 2 tablespoons of the batter onto the skimmer and wait for the batter to fall through the holes into the hot oil to form little balls. You may need to adjust the consistency of the batter, adding more flour or water: if it falls too quickly it is too thin and will not form balls; too thick and it will not go through. Don't force the batter through the holes, although you can give it a hard tap if the batter is flowing too slowly. Fry the boondis for 30–40 seconds. Use another spoon (or skimmer if you have one) to remove the boondis and spread them on a plate. Wash the skimmer in between each drop-making cycle.

Once all the boondis have been fried, add the saffron strands and colour, if using, to the sugar syrup and warm it over a low heat. Drop all the boondis into the warm syrup and stir to coat them well. Ideally, leave them in the syrup overnight, stirring a few times to ensure that all the drops get to absorb the syrup. If you want to give these as a gift, take them out of the syrup using a slotted spoon.

# Coconut Ladoo

A twist on the traditional Bengali *narkel naru* (coconut *ladoo*), which is often made with jaggery. Bengalis are known for their love of *mishti* (sweets). Every locality has its much-cherished sweet shops and it is not unusual to see a queue of people outside the sweet shop at tea time waiting to buy hot *shingaras* (a Bengali style of samosa) and *jalebis* (a spiral-shaped, syrup-soaked sweet). However, coconut *ladoo* is not something people would usually buy in a sweet shop – it is a very traditional family dessert made at home on auspicious occasions, usually by the women of the house. Our neighbours in Calcutta would make these for the festivals of *Lakshmi Puja* and *Bhai Phonta*, and share them with us.

## INGREDIENTS

200g freshly grated coconut (or you can use frozen)

200g caster sugar

100ml full-fat milk, warmed

½ tsp ground cardamom

2 tsp chopped nuts, such as pistachios, almonds or walnuts (the nuts would vary depending on what was in the home at the time)

rose petals, lavender or marigold flowers,

SERVES 6

to decorate

## METHOD

Heat a heavy-based pan over a medium–high heat, add the coconut and sugar and cook for around 10 minutes until they come together.

Reduce the heat to low, add the warm (not boiling) milk, cardamom and chopped nuts and continue to cook until the milk has been absorbed, which may take 10–15 minutes. You can check if the mixture is ready by spooning a small amount onto a plate and rolling it: if it rolls easily, it is ready. Otherwise, continue to cook over a low heat until ready.

Leave the mixture until cool enough to handle comfortably. Roll the ladoos into 12 or 18 balls, depending on your preference, and decorate with flower petals.

# Cooking Lessons

the dishes that taught me
how to cook

**Returning to live in Calcutta** in 1977 was a turning point for my mother. My sister Amna was almost ten years old, I was eight and my brother Arif was five, and we witnessed the gradual transformation of my mother from a housewife to a businesswoman.

Initially, Ammu wanted to start a cookery school. She planned to hold the classes in the house when my father was at work and we were in school (so similar, the way Ammu and I both began our food careers from the home). The leaflets for the cooking classes were prepared and then my mother got an unexpected opportunity. My grandfather, who was a senior director at Tata Steel, asked my mother to cater for a party at his home. Lazeez Catering was born that night (*lazeez* means delectable and delicious in Urdu). The cooking school never happened. Instead, my mother started a catering business and within a year she was a towering figure in the Calcutta food scene. She was catering at the iconic Tollygunge Club, at the Royal Calcutta Turf Club, and for parties and weddings. She was the first female entrepreneur in the family.

I would spend a lot of my time in the kitchen with my mother while she supervised the food. She would make me taste the dishes and ask me if a dish needed more seasoning. She would give instructions to the cooks, watching carefully to ensure everything was cooked properly. This decade I spent at home, accompanying my mother to the bazaar, the fish market and the spice shops, was an education in itself. I did not know how to cook but was immersed in a kitchen environment where my mother was constantly giving oral instructions to the cooks and assistants. I was with her when she designed menus with clients. Later, she would explain to me why she suggested certain dishes, what worked well together and what was practical for the kitchen to cook. She always seemed so unhurried. She never lost her temper. She forgave easily and held no grudges. I would argue with her not to re-employ someone who had let her down in the past, but she would smile and tell me that she had to give people a second chance, never to burn bridges, as a day may come when she will need forgiveness. She was deeply spiritual and she saw her business as a vehicle for good. She continued to financially support all her staff in their retirement and would stand by and hire women who were accused of being 'fallen'. In her gentle, non-judgemental way, she embraced those who society had abandoned and gave them a job. To some extent, Darjeeling Express is an extension of Ammu's business.

Top right: Ammu cooking in our tiny Cambridge kitchen on her first visit to see me after my marriage. She inaugurated the pot we had bought in anticipation of her arrival!

Top left: Ammu, Phopoo Jani (my father's sister) and me. Ammu and Phopoo Jani were friends before my mother married my father. This was a rare meeting, as travel between India and Pakistan was difficult, so we all met up in London. My aunt was not very well, and Ammu knew she would insist on cooking if my mother did, so we bought food from Marks & Spencer and spent the evenings chatting and not doing any cooking or washing up. This was why my aunt had not realised I could not cook until she saw me again after my marriage!

Bottom left: My mother had a beautiful collection of well-washed cotton kaftans, which she would keep for us to wear at home. We would wear soft cotton kaftans and spend our days sitting on Ammu's bed and talking.

Bottom right: Ammu in Holland Park on a visit to England.

Although I left home without knowing how to cook, I was clearly very knowledgeable about food without realising it. When I eventually had my first cooking lesson in my early twenties in the Lazeez Catering kitchen, I had a large audience. I was watched by an assortment of street dogs, house cats and all of the Lazeez team. The moment I started cooking, it was as though waves of memories of all I had heard in the kitchen in the past hit me. The instructions Ammu gave me as I cooked blended in with all my memories of watching the dish – the *Shami Kabab*, page 110 – being cooked before. When the food was ready, my mother tasted it and approved, then served it to all the staff who had been watching. Haji Saheb called out, 'May Allah bless your hands'. On hard days, I remember that comment and it always comforts me.

My marriage was arranged in a whirlwind. I was engaged in September and married a few weeks later by mid-December. Most of the weeks building up to the wedding were spent in organising the menu and the considerable logistics of accommodating the huge numbers of the wedding party. Learning to cook was somehow not a priority, especially after my future husband told me he did not believe in gender roles and would cook for me (he never mentioned his repertoire and ability were extremely limited!). I hurriedly wrote down some notes on how to cook in my diary while hanging around the kitchen – random lists of ingredients and instructions, which I thought would be useful. I had not seen an Indian cookbook before. I did not know how recipes were written! I never realised how precious those scribbled notes would become when I left home. Memories of the conversations in the kitchen between Ammu and the cooks, combined with the notes in my diary, were the first steps to my cooking journey. The diary had been a silent witness to Ammu's cooking and had been in my family kitchen and immersed in the aromas of my home. In a barren and cold new land, the diary was my companion.

I had not completely understood how my life was going to change when I headed to Cambridge. I took the food I ate at home for granted. I had never left home before – I did not know what it would be like to be without Ammu. For a brief time, I had the company of my father's sister Phopoo Jani in England. She was a wonderful person and a brilliant cook and was appalled that I did not know how to cook when I arrived. She promised my mother she would teach me the basics.

This chapter follows the path Phopoo Jani took with me in my early cooking lessons. The recipes include ingredients that were easily available in Cambridge in the 1990s and I have selected recipes that are good starting points if you are new to cooking Indian food. The *Hariyali Murgh* (page 98) has a very traditional marinade but is easy to oven-cook. The Mini Lamb Koftas (pages 78–9) and Masala Fish Fry (page 80) are both dishes where you can trial and test by cooking a piece first, so it is much easier to learn to adjust seasoning, the heat of the oil and see how long it takes to cook. The *Malpua* (page 116) is similar to making a pancake. I hope that after cooking the recipes from this chapter you are a more confident Indian cook! Once I could cook with more confidence, I was ready to start recreating the dishes I yearned for.

Watching Ammu cook in Cambridge was a game-changer.
I realised the aromas and flavours of my home in India
could be transported to another land, and that it was the
rhythm of cooking that was important. Like an old song,
I knew all the words, I just had not written them down.
As I watched Ammu cook, I knew I could do it too.

# Mini Lamb Koftas with Mint Yoghurt Dip

SERVES 6–8

These mini lamb koftas were one of the first dishes I learned to cook. If you are new to Indian cooking, this is a good dish to start with. One advantage is that you can test the mix by frying one ball and then tasting it. It's also good practice for your kofta-rolling technique, and working out how to ensure they do not break. Traditionally, the distinction between a kabab and a kofta is that a kabab does not have any gravy with it, while a kofta does. In this case there is no gravy, but the mixture is rolled into a ball, the shape most often associated with koftas. I have suggested mixing beef with lamb mince to get an interesting texture, but you can use just one meat or experiment with others. I would serve this as a starter ahead of dinner or even at a barbecue. You could also serve with sharing dishes – it would be delicious with Karai Baingan (Aubergine Fritters, page 100) and Rose, Apricot and Pistachio Pulao (page 212).

## INGREDIENTS

500g minced beef (10 per cent fat)

250g lean minced lamb

200g onions, finely chopped

4-cm piece of fresh ginger, grated

4 garlic cloves, finely chopped

1½ tsp salt

1 tsp ground black pepper

½ tsp ground turmeric

1 tsp chilli powder

2 green chillies, finely chopped

1 tsp chaat masala (see Note opposite)

2 eggs, beaten

vegetable oil, for deep-frying

2 slices white bread (if needed)

*Mint Yoghurt Dip*

200ml full-fat yoghurt or crème fraîche

handful of fresh mint leaves, chopped

½ lemon, for squeezing

## METHOD

Combine all the kofta ingredients (except the oil and bread) in a bowl. Cover and set aside for 30 minutes.

To make the dip, mix the yoghurt or crème fraîche with the mint, a generous pinch of salt and a squeeze of lemon juice. Chill.

Before you shape all the koftas it is a good idea to test-fry one or two to check for seasoning. Oil your hands and roll a piece of the mixture into a 2.5cm diameter ball, rolling it tightly so it doesn't break when you fry it and smoothing over any cracks.

Heat 10cm of oil in a deep pan or wok over a high heat. If you have a deep fryer you can use that. Once the oil is hot, reduce the heat

to medium and add your first kofta, turning it frequently, for 4–5 minutes until cooked through. Taste and adjust the seasoning. If the kofta breaks when you fry it, briefly soak the bread in cold water, then squeeze out all the liquid. Break the bread into small lumps and mix into the meat mixture. After adding the bread, wait for 15 minutes before you start rolling the koftas again.

Roll the mixture into 2.5cm diameter balls as described. As you make them, keep them tightly covered so they do not dry out while you roll the remainder of the mixture. You can keep them, covered, in the fridge for 2–3 hours.

Fry the balls in a single layer, in batches, turning them around frequently to ensure they cook evenly.

Serve the koftas with cocktail sticks and the mint yoghurt dip.

**Note** Chaat masala is a tangy spice blend that can be added to recipes or sprinkled on top as a seasoning. You can find it in Asian food shops.

# Masala Fish Fry

## Spicy Marinated Fish Fillets

This spiced fried fish should be eaten freshly cooked. Cutting the fish into strips should prevent it from breaking up when you fry it, but even if it does break up, it is still going to taste delicious. You can minimise the chances of the fish flaking by frying a few pieces at a time. My mother would always instruct the cooks frying the fish not to rush, to be patient and let one side seal before carefully and gently turning the fish to cook the other side. When I was learning to cook, I would fry just one piece at a time and that way I had enough room to turn the fish without it breaking by touching another piece. Ideally, use a flat, thin spoon or spatula to turn the fish. My mother would never stop me from eating the occasional piece that broke when frying, and on days when each piece stayed intact, she would give me one, saying 'this one has your name written on it'!

This is a great dish to make if you have friends and family coming over for a summer meal outdoors, as there is no gravy. It also goes with any kind of salad or greens. You can use any firm white fish for it.

### INGREDIENTS

8 skinless haddock fillets

4 garlic cloves, crushed

1 large green chilli, finely chopped

1½ tsp ground turmeric

3 tsp ground coriander

6 tbsp vinegar

2 tsp salt

vegetable oil, for frying

chilli flakes, to garnish

2 limes, cut into wedges, to serve

### METHOD

Cut the fish into evenly sized strips, about 2.5cm wide. The strips should be cut at an angle and against the grain. This should prevent the fish from breaking when you fry it.

In a bowl, combine the garlic, green chilli, turmeric and coriander with the vinegar and salt to make a paste. Add the fish and marinate for 20 minutes.

Heat a 2cm depth of oil in a non-stick frying pan over a medium–high heat. Shallow-fry the fish, a few pieces at a time. The fish will spit and crackle when you put it into the oil, so keep a safe distance. As the fish is cooked, remove from the pan and set aside while you cook the remaining pieces.

When all the fish is cooked, sprinkle with chilli flakes and serve with lime wedges.

# Chapati

## Wholemeal Bread

This is the everyday bread eaten by many families in India. Chapati flour is readily available in many Asian shops and also in mainstream supermarkets. If you can't find it, you can use sifted wholemeal flour. Weigh the flour after sifting and discarding the bran left in the sieve.

In some parts of India, the chapatis would be cooked and wrapped in a clean cloth and put into a closed basket or tin and taken to the dinner table. As the bread cools it becomes hard, so it is a bread that is meant to be eaten hot and immediately. Some of our food has uncomfortable roots of patriarchy. Historically, there was a culture where the men and boys of the family ate first, while the women and girls ate later – in many families it was the women and girls who were making the hot chapatis that were served to the men. Many years later, talking to friends about gender bias, I heard references to the burnt chapatis that were given to them – the rejects.

If you want to cook the chapatis in advance, so you can sit and break bread with your family and friends, you need to cook them on low–medium heat so they remain soft. Wrap them in a cloth immediately. If you cook the chapatis until they develop dark brown spots, they will harden if you keep them. To honour the memories of all those generations of women and girls who never broke bread at the table with their families, please do make these and share with your loved ones.

Enjoy with Navratan Korma (Nine-Jewel Korma, page 210) or Karai Murgh (Chicken and Onion Cooked in a Karai, page 202).

### INGREDIENTS

225g sifted chapati flour (*atta/chakki atta*) or wholemeal flour, plus extra for dusting

¼ tsp salt

150ml cold water

### METHOD

Put the flour and salt in a bowl and gradually add the water, kneading as you go, to make a soft but pliable dough. This may take 5–7 minutes.

Transfer the dough to a lightly floured surface and knead using strong downward pressure for about 5 minutes. Cover the dough and set aside for 30 minutes.

Divide the dough into six equal pieces and shape each piece into a ball. Flatten to a disc and roll out on a lightly floured surface until each piece is 15cm in diameter.

Heat a *tawa* or frying pan over a medium–high heat and cook one chapati at a time, pressing down on the edges with scrunched-up kitchen paper or a clean kitchen cloth. The bread should puff up and be flecked with brown, which is the sign it is ready to eat.

Top left: My grandmother with her eldest girls. My mother is the little one.

Middle far left: My oldest aunt carrying Ammu.

Bottom left: She is not visible in the picture but that hand holding me steady is that of my mother. This is one of the few pictures I have seen in the family archive of me on my own.

Bottom right: My parents, a few weeks after their wedding in 1967. In contrast to the family life my father had (he spent most of his childhood with his grandfather Bapu), my mother was raised in a big clan. My father took to large family feasts and intense conversations about food at the table like a duck to water.

Middle left: A rare picture of both sets of grandparents with my sister Amna as a baby.

Above middle: Perched on the balustrade in front of the Victoria memorial in Calcutta is Ammu, flanked by her older sisters. My grandparents would take all the grandchildren for a walk here as part of their daily exercise routine. Sadly, we were not allowed to eat the hot onion pakoras or *chaat* sold by street vendors outside the gates! My grandfather would buy us cups of vanilla ice cream to share.

Above right: Nani, my maternal grandmother.

Right: Ammu with her sister, Bhutun Khala.

# Palong Shak Chingri

## Bengali-style Prawns with Spinach

SERVES 4

This is a traditional Bengali recipe. The food of Bengal was largely composed of fresh seafood, rice and vegetables. Combining seasonal vegetables with seafood or meat was very popular. The humidity from the delta of the Bay of Bengal and long hot days was probably the reason why so much Bengali food was so fresh and quickly cooked.

Ammu ate a lot more Bengali food than my father or us, as this was part of her heritage. It was an occasional treat for my mother to have the kitchen make something that only she enjoyed. This dish was something that was made for lunch, as my father would be at work, so it was usually just my mother and one of us eating at home.

This is also a good dish to make if you are entertaining, as serving prawns is a bit of an extravagance. However, mixed with spinach, which is cheaper, the combination looks lovely. Although this is traditionally made with smaller and cheaper shrimps in most households in Bengal, you can buy larger prawns and make this a centrepiece dish on your table when you have a party.

### INGREDIENTS

330g raw peeled king prawns

½ tsp ground turmeric

¼ tsp chilli powder

4 tbsp vegetable oil

2 brown onions, thinly sliced into half moons

2 tbsp ginger paste

1 tbsp garlic paste

4 fresh red chillies: 3 finely chopped; 1, sliced, to garnish

900g fresh spinach leaves

1 tsp salt

### METHOD

Devein the prawns, rinse and pat dry with kitchen paper. Rub the turmeric and chilli powder on the prawns and set aside.

Heat the oil in a pan over a high heat, add the prawns and stir-fry until they just turn opaque (do not overcook) then remove using a slotted spoon and place on a plate.

Add the onions to the pan and fry over a medium heat until the edges start to brown. Add the ginger and garlic pastes and the chopped chillies and fry until the oil separates from the onion mixture. Add the spinach and salt and cook until the water released from the spinach has evaporated.

Return the prawns to the pan with the spinach mixture and cook for a couple more minutes. Taste and adjust the seasoning, adding more salt if required. Serve immediately, garnished with sliced red chilli.

# Baingan Pakora

## Aubergine Fritters

Pakoras and monsoon are synonymous for me! There is something so comforting in eating crispy fried things when the rain has halted play! In Bengal and Bangladesh, these are called *beguni* and the recipe is similar. To check that the batter and seasoning is correct, fry one and taste it before making the rest. The consistency of the batter should be like a pancake batter. When you dip the aubergine, make sure it is fully covered. If you cannot make a chutney to accompany the pakora, you can serve it with tomato ketchup or any chilli sauce or dipping sauce you have at home. A delicious snack or starter to share.

### INGREDIENTS

300g aubergine (1 medium aubergine)

salt, for sprinkling

200ml vegetable oil

*Batter*

125g gram flour (besan)

½ tsp salt

¼ tsp ground turmeric

¼ tsp chilli powder

pinch of asafoetida (optional)

200ml water

### METHOD

Cut the aubergine into slices, about 5mm thick, and spread on a large plate or tray. Sprinkle salt on both sides and set aside.

Start heating the oil in a wok or *karai* over a low–medium heat.

To make the batter, mix the gram flour, salt, turmeric, chilli powder and asafoetida, if using, in a bowl. Gradually whisk in the water to make a smooth thick batter.

Gently squeeze the aubergine slices to remove any moisture.

Raise the heat under the wok to high. Dip two aubergine slices at a time into the batter to coat them completely, then fry in the hot oil, turning once, until crisp on both sides. Drain on kitchen paper while you fry the remaining aubergine slices. Serve hot.

*Pictured with Kancha Aamer Chutney (Raw Mango Chutney, page 158).*

# Sabit Masoor Dal

## Brown Lentils

SERVES 6

Dals, or pulses, are an important source of protein for many Indian families. It is true to say that, irrespective of food preferences, everybody in India eats a lot of dal. The split version of the brown lentil is confusingly called red lentil. Brown lentils do take longer to cook than the split ones, but they have a nice nutty flavour and more vitamins than the split skinless lentils.

This is a versatile dish, to be served with rice or bread. You can cook the lentils one or two days in advance, adding the temper at the last minute. It goes well with gooseberry chutney (page 62). When my son Ariz began training to box, he was very keen to have a lot more protein. This dal was one of his favourites – he would often eat it cold from the fridge as a salad with chutney on the side. I prefer it warm.

### INGREDIENTS

350g brown lentils

1 tsp ground turmeric

2.5-cm piece of fresh ginger, grated

3 green chillies

1 onion, finely chopped

1.5 litres warm water

1½ tsp salt

1 tbsp tomato purée

### Temper

4 tbsp ghee or oil

4 dried red chillies

1 tsp cumin seeds

4 garlic cloves, cut in half

½ onion, thinly sliced

### METHOD

Wash the lentils and soak in cold water for 2 hours.

Drain the lentils and place in a heavy-based pan with a tight-fitting lid. Add the turmeric, ginger, chillies and onion, followed by the water, and bring to the boil. Cover the pan, reduce the heat and simmer for 45 minutes or until the lentils have softened. Stir occasionally to ensure they are not sticking to the base of the pan. If this is the first time you have cooked brown lentils, don't expect the texture to be like split lentils or even chickpeas: the whole lentil will hold its shape.

Once the lentils are cooked, add the salt and tomato purée and cook, uncovered, over a medium–low heat for about 20 minutes until everything cooks down and thickens. If at any point the dal is drying out, add a splash of water. Once the lentils are ready, remove from the heat while you prepare the temper.

In a small frying pan, heat the ghee or oil over a high heat. Working very quickly so the ingredients do not burn, add the dried chillies, cumin seeds and garlic, and finally the onion. Cook for a few minutes until the garlic turns brown, then pour the tempering oil and spices over the warm dal in the pan.

# Machher Mamlet

## Fish Omelette

SERVES 4

Omelettes are called *mamlets* in Bengal. I do not know why! For many Bengalis, a classic comfort meal is *dim bhaja bhaat* – like eggs and toast but in this case it is eggs with boiled rice. This version of spiced omelette has a fish and onion stuffing. If you do not eat fish, you can replace the fish with another filling, such as *Chennar Mattar Bhurji* (page 264). Another way to make this dish is to cook it like a Spanish omelette. The older generation in Bengal, who grew up at a time when eggs were not easily available (unless you had your own chickens), treated eggs as a luxury and this may explain why in many Bengali households eggs are not just eaten for breakfast but as a main meal. We eat this as a main meal rather than for breakfast – a simple but delicious one for busy evenings.

### INGREDIENTS

400g firm white skinless fish fillet

4 tbsp butter

1 large onion, thinly sliced

4 garlic cloves, finely chopped

¼ tsp ground turmeric

½ tsp ground black pepper

¼ tsp chilli powder

1 tsp salt

8 large eggs, beaten

4 tbsp chopped fresh coriander

### METHOD

Poach the fish in water until it is just cooked then break into chunks and set aside.

Heat the butter in a non-stick frying pan over a medium–high heat. Add the onion and garlic and stir for a minute, then add the turmeric, black pepper, chilli powder and salt and stir for another minute. Add the fish and gently stir to coat it with the spiced onions and garlic. Remove the mixture from the pan and set aside while you make the omelette.

Wipe out the pan with kitchen paper and put it back over a medium–high heat, adding a little more butter if needed. Add the eggs and most of the coriander and cook until almost set. Put the fish filling on one half of the omelette, fold the other half over and serve immediately, sprinkled with the reamaining coriander.

# Aloo Gobi Mattar

## Potatoes, Cauliflower and Peas

SERVES 4–6

I love peas. Cauliflower and peas are both winter vegetables and this dish was something we would make at home for family gatherings. We had a lot of relatives in my mother's family who were completely averse to eating any vegetables, but were always tempted by this dish. It was the only one where Ammu would make enough for everyone in the party. All other vegetable dishes were made in small portions for the occasional vegetarian among our guests.

This is a crowd-pleaser and not just for vegan or vegetarian guests! The combination of the three different textures make this dish ideal as an accompaniment to meat dishes or as a single main for a plant-based meal.

### INGREDIENTS

300g cauliflower florets

200g new or salad potatoes

½ tsp cumin seeds

6 tbsp vegetable oil

2 dried red chillies

1 onion, roughly chopped

3 large garlic cloves, crushed

1-cm piece of fresh ginger, finely chopped or grated

¼ tsp ground turmeric

225g tinned plum tomatoes

¾ tsp salt

¼ tsp sugar (optional)

150g frozen peas, defrosted

2 spicy green chillies, cut in half

2 tbsp chopped fresh coriander leaves

### METHOD

Cut the cauliflower florets into evenly sized pieces, about 4cm wide, so they all cook at the same rate. Scrub the potatoes clean, leaving the skins on, and cut them into 2-cm cubes.

Dry roast the cumin seeds in a heavy-based pan over a low heat, stirring until they turn a few shades darker. Tip them onto a plate and leave to cool. Grind to a powder, using a spice grinder or a pestle and mortar.

Heat the oil in a *karai* or deep pan over a medium–high heat. Add the dried chillies and stir for a few seconds; as soon as they darken, remove to a plate and set aside. Add the cauliflower in batches and fry until the florets begin to brown at the edges. Using a slotted spoon, remove to a plate. Next, fry the potatoes in batches until they begin to brown, then remove with a slotted spoon, leaving as much oil in the pan as possible.

Add the onion to the pan and stir for a few minutes until it begins to brown. Add the garlic and ginger, followed by the turmeric, stirring continuously to prevent the onion from sticking. Next, add the tomatoes, followed by the fried red chillies. Add the salt and sugar, if using, stirring at regular intervals

for 4–5 minutes, until you can see the oil coming to the edge of the tomato mixture.

Put the cauliflower and potatoes back in the pan. Do not cover. If the mixture is sticking to the base of the pan, add a couple of tablespoons of water. Stir to coat the cauliflower and potatoes with the spicy tomato mix. Reduce

the heat to medium–low and simmer for 3–4 minutes until the cauliflower and potatoes are almost cooked.

Add the peas and the green chillies and simmer until the peas are cooked. To serve, sprinkle the ground roasted cumin seeds and fresh coriander on top.

# Mattar Paratha

## Paratha Stuffed with Peas

Learning to make stuffed parathas can be a life-changing skill! Anything from mashed potatoes to minced meat to crumbled paneer can be stuffed inside a paratha to make a satisfying meal, so use this recipe and play around with the stuffings. It is important that the stuffing does not have any sharp bits or rough edges that will tear the paratha when you roll it. I like eating this with yoghurt on the side.

### INGREDIENTS

200g chapati flour (*atta/chakki atta*) or wholemeal flour

100g plain flour, plus extra for dusting

1 tsp salt

about 200ml warm water

120g shelled peas

1 green chilli, finely chopped (optional)

1 tbsp chopped fresh coriander

3 tbsp melted ghee or unsalted butter (or vegetable oil)

SERVES 8

### METHOD

Mix both the flours in a bowl and add ½ teaspoon of the salt. Make a well in the centre and gradually add the warm water. Knead until you have a soft but pliable dough. Cover the bowl with a damp cloth and set aside for 2 hours.

Boil the peas then drain and mash with the chilli, if using, the coriander and the remaining ½ teaspoon salt. Divide into eight equal portions and set aside.

Divide the dough into eight equal pieces and shape each piece into a ball. On a lightly floured surface, roll out each piece to form a 12cm circle, sprinkling flour over the dough as you roll. Put a portion of the pea mix in the middle of each circle of dough and lift the edges together to form a sack. Seal the tip and shape the dough into a ball again. This time you need to be careful as there is a stuffing inside.

Flatten each stuffed dough ball on the floured surface and gently roll out to make a 15–20cm circle. Do not use pressure while rolling as you don't want to tear the surface of the parathas.

Heat a *tawa* or frying pan over a low heat. Cook one paratha at a time for 4–5 minutes on each side until golden brown. Drizzle over a little melted ghee, butter or oil as you cook each side. Serve warm.

*Pictured with Lal (Red) Chutney (page 34).*

# Hariyali Murgh

## Baked Chicken Thighs with Herbs

SERVES 6

*Hariyali* means greenery in Hindi but it also has a more nuanced cultural meaning: it is often used as a term of blessing. Elders would touch the head of a child, saying '*Tere taqdeer mein hariyali bhar ke aaye, tum phoolon phalo*' – may you thrive and flourish. It was a blessing of abundance.

This was one of the first dishes I learned to cook when I came to England, as the butcher in Cambridge sold skinned chicken thighs. In India, we rarely eat chicken with the skin on, as the masalas can penetrate the meat more easily without it. So, I was surprised to see chicken sold with the skin on it in England. I struggled when taking the skin off until someone told me to use kitchen paper to grab the skin to pull it off. I serve this with Khaas Aloo (Special Potatoes, page 208) and any type of bread.

### INGREDIENTS

12 skinless chicken thighs, on the bone

3 tsp salt

50g butter

1 lime, sliced, to serve

*Marinade*

50g fresh coriander leaves and stalks, chopped

50g fresh mint leaves, chopped

5 green chillies (not the bird's eye variety, which are too fiery)

300ml full-fat Greek-style yoghurt

### METHOD

To make the marinade, use a hand blender to blend the chopped herbs and chillies with the yoghurt.

Put the chicken in a bowl, add the marinade to cover completely, then cover the bowl and leave in the fridge for at least 2 hours, preferably 6 hours, or overnight. Remove from the fridge at least 30 minutes before cooking.

Preheat the oven to 180°C/160°C fan/gas 4. Line a roasting tin with a large piece of foil.

Season the marinated chicken with the salt and place in the lined roasting tin. Dot with the butter. Fold the foil over the chicken and bake for 1½ hours.

Open up the foil and cook for a further 15 minutes to reduce the liquid. Serve with slices of lime.

# Karai Baingan

## Stir-fried Aubergines

Unlike vegetables such as tomatoes, potatoes and chillies, which were introduced to India by the Portuguese, aubergine was native to India but was referred to by a Portuguese name: *bringal* (*berinjela*). When I moved to the UK, I had never heard the word aubergine or eggplant. When an American student in Cambridge called it an eggplant I was mystified: how could a purple elongated vegetable resemble an egg? Years later, I saw my first round white aubergine in Borough Market and the mystery became clear. This dish goes really well with rice and bread. If it is a very warm day, it does taste nice cold, too.

### INGREDIENTS

9 tbsp vegetable oil

1 large onion, thinly sliced

1kg (about 3 medium) aubergines, cut into 2.5-cm cubes

1 red pepper, cut into 2-cm cubes

1 large tomato, cut into 2-cm cubes

2 tbsp ginger paste

1 tbsp garlic paste

1 tsp chilli powder

1 tsp ground turmeric

2 tsp ground coriander

1 heaped tsp salt

200ml full-fat Greek-style yoghurt

2 tbsp fresh lemon juice

SERVES 6

### *To Garnish*

small handful of fresh coriander leaves, chopped

a few green chillies, left whole or roughly chopped (optional)

### METHOD

In a large frying pan, *karai* or wok, heat the oil over a medium–high heat. Add the onion and fry, stirring occasionally, for about 10 minutes until golden brown and caramelised. Using a slotted spoon, remove the onion from the pan, leaving as much of the oil in the pan as possible, and place on a plate to drain. Spread the onion across the plate so it crisps as it cools.

Add the aubergines to the pan, followed by the red pepper. Stir-fry for a minute, then add the tomato, ginger and garlic pastes, chilli powder, turmeric, ground coriander, salt and yoghurt. Turn up the heat to high and cook for 5 minutes, stirring continuously. Lower the heat to medium–high, add the caramelised onion and cook for a further 5 minutes, then add the lemon juice. Taste to check the seasoning and adjust as necessary.

Before serving, garnish with the coriander and green chillies, if using. If you do not want to make the dish spicier, keep the chillies whole. If you want to add some extra heat, roughly chop the chillies.

# Apple, Chilli and Walnut Chutney

SERVES 4–6

It was rare to get a large variety of apples when I was young. Most of the apples in India grew in Kashmir, Himachal Pradesh and other faraway regions. Whenever we were gifted apples by visitors we invariably got walnuts too, as they were also grown in Kashmir. I was very fortunate to spend my childhood visiting and eating at the home of Namrata Razdan, who was my sister Amna's best friend, but they kindly allowed me to hang around with them. We spent long afternoons drinking Kashmiri chai in Namrata's house, chatting about life and our dreams! This is my homage to that friendship and the beautiful land of Kashmir.

This chutney goes particularly well with Bharwan Kofta (Stuffed Meat Kofta, page 130), Lamb Seekh Kabab (page 242) or Chingri Chop (Prawn Croquettes, page 108).

## INGREDIENTS

2 tbsp ghee or unsalted butter

2.5-cm piece of cinnamon stick

¼ tsp fennel seeds

1 clove

2 dried red chillies

1 green cardamom pod, crushed open

6 tart apples, peeled, cored and thinly sliced

¼ tsp cayenne pepper

80ml orange juice

110g soft brown sugar

40g walnuts, toasted and roughly chopped

## METHOD

Heat the ghee or butter in a large non-stick pan over a medium heat. Add the cinnamon stick, fennel seeds, clove, dried chillies and cardamom pod, and stir until the spices darken slightly and the butter is frothing. Add the apples, cayenne pepper, orange juice and sugar.

Reduce the heat to medium–low. Cook for 30 minutes, stirring towards the end of the cooking time to ensure it is not sticking to the base of the pan. Once the chutney is thick and shiny, take the pan off the heat and stir in the walnuts. Serve warm or at room temperature.

This can be kept in a sealed container in the fridge for up to 5 days.

# Baghare Aloo

## Potatoes with Dried Red Chillies

This is a delicious and quick potato dish that can accompany any meal. It is important to get the right potatoes for this dish: it does not work as well with new potatoes or with floury potatoes – you need to find that perfect in-between potato that will soften but not break up in cooking. When slicing the potatoes, the actual thickness is less important, but all the slices must be even. This way, all the potatoes will cook at the same time and you will not have a mix of very soft and crumbled potatoes with some that are not completely cooked. Start with the smaller amount of chillies, as not everyone can tolerate high chilli heat.

This was a staple at our family table when I was a child. My maternal grandmother would often eat this for breakfast with fried puris, which does seem very indulgent, but it is a good combination. Try it with Zaffran Rogni Roti (Saffron-infused Bread, page 224).

SERVES 6

INGREDIENTS

1kg white potatoes, cut in half and thinly sliced

4 tbsp vegetable oil

4–6 dried red chillies, broken in half

1 tsp ground turmeric

1½ tsp salt

METHOD

To prevent the potatoes from sticking to each other, soak the slices in a bowl of cold water for 10 minutes and then rinse under cold running water to remove any excess starch. Dry the potatoes on kitchen paper.

Heat the oil in a wide frying pan over a medium–high heat. Add the broken chillies and stir for a few seconds until they darken. Add the potatoes and spread them out in the pan. Add the turmeric and salt and stir for a minute before lowering the heat.

Gently cook, uncovered, over a low heat for about 5–6 minutes (the time will need to be increased if the slices are thicker). Shake the pan and stir gently to ensure the potatoes cook evenly without breaking. But don't worry if the potato slices do start to break up – it will still taste delicious.

# Mishti Kumro

## Pumpkin with Red Chillies

SERVES 6–8

In Bengal, the most prized pumpkin is *mishti kumro*, a sweet variety with deep orange flesh; a good alternative is kabocha squash, although any kind of squash which is in season is perfect for this dish. The *panch phoran* (Bengali five-seed spice mix) can be replaced with black mustard seeds. The heat of the dried red chillies and a touch of sugar perfectly balance the flavours in this pumpkin dish. If you are not a fan of any kind of squash, you could replace it with parsnips: cut them into cubes and par-boil them, before following the recipe.

If you wanted to have a quintessential Bengali meal, *mishti kumro* would have to be one of the dishes I would recommend from this book – together with the Machher Dopiyaza (Fish with Double Onions, page 200) or Machher Korma (Fish Korma, page 52) and accompanied with rice and a *bharta* (see page 217). We would have a very Bengali meal at lunchtime on a Friday in Calcutta and it was usually a combination of all of these dishes.

INGREDIENTS

1.2kg pumpkin, peeled and seeded

½ tsp ground turmeric

1½ tsp salt

5 tbsp vegetable oil

1 tsp panch phoran

5 dried red chillies

5 garlic cloves, crushed

½ tsp sugar

METHOD

Cut the pumpkin into 2.5-cm cubes. Rub with the turmeric and salt, then set aside for at least 30 minutes or up to 3 hours.

Heat the oil in a heavy-based pan or frying pan over a medium–high heat. Add the panch phoran, chillies and garlic, and stir for a few seconds.

Add the pumpkin to the pan. It should have enough moisture to prevent sticking, but if not, add a splash of water. Stir the pumpkin to coat it in the spices, then lower the heat and cover the pan. Simmer for about 15 minutes until tender, stirring from time to time using a flat metal spoon or spatula and gently taking the spoon under the pumpkin, turning it carefully to ensure it does not disintegrate.

Once the pumpkin is cooked, stir in the sugar and serve hot.

# Chingri Chop

## Prawn Croquettes

One interesting aspect of the British and Portuguese influences on Bengal's culinary heritage has been an array of deep-fried chops, cutlets and croquettes, which were initially limited to the more elite railway meals in the colonial era. Slowly, the passion to coat in breadcrumbs and deep-fry food – mashed potatoes, minced mutton, beetroot, prawns – spread to the general public. My favourite is a vegetable chop I would buy on my train journey from Calcutta to Jamshedpur – the vendor would call it 'cut-lass' (cutlet). The reason the recipe is not in the book is because I have not been able to replicate it from memory. Luckily, this chingri chop is a recipe I could get from my mother. Hope you enjoy it!

### INGREDIENTS

1kg raw peeled small prawns

1 tsp white pepper

1½ tsp salt

4 slices white bread, crusts removed

60g white onion, finely chopped

4 garlic cloves, finely chopped

4 green chillies, finely chopped

2 tsp fresh lime juice

4 tbsp finely chopped fresh coriander leaves

vegetable oil, for deep-frying

### SERVES 8

### METHOD

Chop the prawns into small pieces, but not too finely. Put them in a bowl and stir in the white pepper and salt.

Soak the bread in cold water, then squeeze out all the liquid, break it into small lumps and place in a bowl. Add the onion, garlic, chillies, lime juice and coriander and knead until evenly combined. Add the prawns and mix until evenly distributed.

Heat the oil in a deep fryer or a heavy-based pan over a medium–high heat. Shape a piece of the mixture into a 5-cm croquette and test-fry one croquette; when cool enough to eat, taste and adjust the seasoning, adding more salt, pepper or lime juice if required.

Shape the remaining mixture into 5-cm croquettes and fry in the hot oil in small batches, turning frequently, for 2–3 minutes. Drain on kitchen paper.

Serve with any dipping sauce you like, such as chilli sauce or tomato ketchup, or serve some *Anaras Jhal Chutney* (page 228) on the side.

# Shami Kabab

## Stuffed Meat Patties

In my home, we always made *shami kabab* with a mix of beef and mutton mince to get the right texture (all mince was called *keema*). My mother preferred to mix the egg with the mixture before cooking, so that's the way I do it. Some of my aunts would coat the meat patty in the beaten egg before frying. This kabab may take a couple of attempts to get right. You can experiment with the mince you use (use just one type of meat if you prefer – chicken is delicious too!). The important thing is to keep the same proportion of meat to dal as in the recipe below.

### INGREDIENTS

500g lean minced beef

500g minced mutton or lamb

200g chana dal (split yellow gram)

50g ginger, peeled and cut into small chunks

50g garlic, cut into chunky pieces

1 tbsp cumin seeds

4 dried red chillies

2.5-cm piece of cinnamon stick

2 green cardamom pods

2 cloves

1 bay leaf

2 tsp salt

3 eggs, beaten

vegetable oil, for shallow frying

### *Stuffing*

4 green chillies, finely chopped

4 tbsp finely chopped red onions

4 tbsp finely chopped mint leaves

### METHOD

Put the meat, dal, ginger, garlic, spices, bay leaf and salt in a deep pan, add enough water to just about cover the mixture, and bring to the boil. Cover and simmer for 30 minutes.

After 30 minutes, remove the lid and cook over a medium heat until all the water has evaporated, using the back of a spoon to break up any lumps. The success of the kabab depends on getting as much of the moisture out as possible. Towards the end of the cooking time, keep stirring to prevent the meat mixture from sticking to the base of the pan.

When the mixture is dry, remove the dried chillies, cinnamon stick, cardamoms, cloves and bay leaf. Transfer the mixture to a food processor, add the eggs and blend to a paste.

Combine the stuffing ingredients in a bowl.

Divide the mixture into 12 equal portions and shape into balls. Make a hollow in the centre of each and fill with a generous pinch of the stuffing. Close the stuffed kabab, bringing the edges together like a pouch and carefully sealing any cracks. Flatten each kabab to form a 5–6cm patty.

Heat the oil in a frying pan over a medium–high heat. Shallow-fry the kababs a few at a time until crisp and brown. Turn them only once: the meat is already cooked, so you are aiming to get a nice crispy brown surface. Serve hot with Zaffran Rogni Roti (page 224) and Lal Chutney (page 34).

*Also pictured on page 163.*

Above and right: My diary with the original handwritten Shami Kabab recipe (see page 110). Stained with age and memories, the diary I carried with me when I left home was my first step to learning how to cook.

Shammi kabab
keema       1 kg ✓
chana dal  200 gms ✓
Adrak      50 gms ✓ sabut
lahsun     50 gms ✓ sabut
red mirchi 10 gms ✓ sabut
garam marala 5 gms ✓
sabit jeera 1 tbs ✓ sabut
eggs        3 pcs
pudina     1 tbs
green chilly 1 tsp
onion      2 tbsp

cook ✓ enough water
to cover till tender. Still
watery - then bhuno -
dry the water - 3 eggs break
make it - taste salt - shred
chilly + mint - stuff it or
mix it in the mixture - press
it - add if knur Ikbal or
most

1.11.89            akhan

उनके जाने के बाद,          रास्ते
इस अन्धेरी रात में,          रौशनी
ना कोई शम्मा जले,
ना कोई मुसाफिर आये,
फिर में किस किस को बताओ,
क्या रौनाक थी इस घर में,
शहर कि रौशनी में भी वह बात
                नहीं थी -
                          ✍

हमारे इस बस्ती में,
रहता है कौन
जिसका नाम हर दिवार और
                दरवाजे
पर लिखवा है
यह कौन दिवाना है
जिसके लिहा पर
खंजर और तलवार को हाल
                इस लिए - गया
बहुत थक गई हूं में
जिन्दगानी से
कोई मुझे उस दिवाने का पता
तो दे दे
                          ✍

# Bhendi Sabzi

## Okra

Cooking okra can be a challenge: if you bruise the vegetable, it will release a glue-like stickiness. The trick is to use a very sharp knife to cut the okra so you do not add extra pressure while cutting them. My advice is ideally to leave the okra whole or cut into big pieces. If you cut them into very tiny pieces, they are best fried to a crisp, which will eliminate the stickiness.

This is a very good side dish to serve when inviting friends or family over for a meal. This was one of the early dishes I learned to cook in Cambridge, closely supervised by my aunt Phopoo Jani, my father's sister who had married and moved to Pakistan and could not come back to India and visit family. When I moved to Cambridge, she was also living in the city for medical treatment and decided that, as I had no cooking skills, she would teach me something very basic. This is the very simple okra dish she taught me. I remember her telling me not to reheat it as it might disintegrate and that it tastes very nice even at room temperature. She sadly passed away a year after teaching me this recipe. I can remember her telling Ammu on the phone that she had taught me a dish that required minimal cutting with a knife as she could see that I was completely unable to cook or use a knife!

SERVES 4

INGREDIENTS

450g okra

4 tbsp vegetable oil

1 onion, chopped

1 large garlic clove, crushed

½ tsp finely grated fresh ginger

1 green chilli, chopped

¾ tsp salt

½ lemon

METHOD

Top and tail the okra. Ideally, they should be around 8cm long. If they are very long, you may need to cut them in half.

Heat the oil in a frying pan over a medium–high heat and fry the okra in batches until just beginning to turn golden brown. You do not want to fully cook them at this stage. Using a slotted spoon and leaving as much oil in the pan as possible, remove the okra and spread out on a plate.

Add the onion to the pan and stir-fry for a minute, then add the garlic, ginger and chilli and cook over a medium–high heat until the raw smell of the garlic has gone.

Put the okra back in the pan, add the salt and just enough water to barely cover the okra. Cook, uncovered, turning the okra frequently until it is cooked. Do not overcook the okra as it will become sticky. Serve with a squeeze of lemon juice.

# Malpua

## Ghee-fried Pancakes Soaked in Syrup

SERVES 4
(2 OR 3 PANCAKES PER PERSON)

This is one of the desserts that is often made for *Holi* – the festival of spring and colour. *Malpua* is very similar to a pancake – the difference is that it is deep-fried in ghee and soaked in syrup! There are many variations of the dish. In eastern India, ripe bananas are mashed and added to the batter; in Bangladesh some families add coconut. This is a plain version, which is more popular in the region where my father comes from. Traditionally in my family, these are decorated with rose petals, which add a wonderful fragrance. As the pancakes are quick to make, I would suggest making the Rabri (Milk Dessert with Pistachio, page 174), too, and creating a truly indulgent dessert by pouring it over the pancakes.

### INGREDIENTS

240g plain flour

180g full-fat Greek-style yoghurt

50:50 ghee and vegetable oil, for deep-frying

*Syrup*

500ml water

250g caster sugar

2 green cardamom pods

rose petals, to garnish (optional)

### METHOD

Sift the flour into a bowl and whisk in the yoghurt to make a smooth batter with the consistency of a thick pancake batter. If it is too thick, you may need to add a little water, whisking in 1 tablespoon at a time. Cover and set aside for an hour.

While the batter is resting, make the syrup. Put the water in a pan with the sugar and cardamom pods and bring to the boil. Keep the liquid at a slow rolling boil until it reduces and thickens slightly, then turn off the heat.

When ready to fry the pancakes, heat an 8cm depth of ghee and oil in a deep frying pan over a medium heat. Drop 1 tablespoon of the batter into the hot oil: it should spread to a pancake shape. Using a slotted spoon, remove from the oil and add to the pan of warm syrup. Repeat until you have used all the batter.

Leave to cool slightly before serving the pancakes drizzled with a little of the syrup and garnished with rose petals, if using.

# Nostalgia

slow cooking to while
away the time

When I finally learned to cook, I knew this was my calling. Not the cooking part, the feeding bit! I felt complete when feeding someone. The feelings of being rootless and lost that I felt during my early years in this country changed when I found I could cook the more nostalgic meals of my childhood that meant so much to me. The food in this chapter celebrates the calm that comes with the process of making something that takes time, requires care and love, but is very much worth it. These recipes are for sharing with friends. We ate these often as a family – hearty meals for colder, rainy months and all-in-one dishes that feel generous without costing a lot of money to make.

My sister Amna got married and left home when I was 16. My fondest food memories were the meals we ate when she would return home to Calcutta with her boys Farhan and Faraz. Once Amna was back, our family felt complete and it was 'us five' again – my parents, my two siblings and me – sitting around our dining table in our Bright Street home in Calcutta. The *Kala Channa* (page 160) and the Methi Chicken (page 152) both remind me of those years when we would eat most of our meals at home so we did not have to drag my nephews around town to eat at restaurants or other family gatherings. Likewise, dishes like the Roast Beef (page 150), Prawn Biryani (page 146) and *Bharwan Kofta* (page 130) were the ones I remembered eating when we were all together. Many of these dishes feed a crowd and sometimes take a little longer than usual. They are slow-cooking dishes to take your time over and are the ones I cook when I want to treat my loved ones and remember those warm feelings of being at home with my family.

I often remember my arrival in Cambridge as a young bride in the early 1990s. Ammu had collected my trousseau over many years. I arrived in a bitter cold January, equipped with beautifully embroidered *shalwar kameez* and woven fine silk sarees. I had several pairs of handmade slippers that matched the embroidery of some of my clothes. Those slippers were never meant for cobblestones and cold rain. Very soon, they all fell apart. I never had the heart to throw them away, as I remember Ammu matching my slippers to my clothes and telling the shoemaker, 'My daughter will look so lovely wearing these'.

When I moved from Calcutta to Cambridge, I felt like the bare trees at the backs of the Cambridge colleges. I felt stripped of everything beautiful and loving. Away from my family and Ammu, I felt exposed

Right: A formal portrait of Bapu, my father's paternal grandfather. Abbu was his favourite grandchild and we have always felt his presence in our lives. A majestic man, Bapu was a significant player in Indian history and politics of the 1930s and '40s. He broke ranks with many of the Muslim nobility and intellectuals who wanted a separate homeland, and believed in keeping India united. Bapu travelled to England as part of the Indian delegation in 1930 to discuss Indian autonomy at the Round Table Conferences. He represented India in the Great Exhibition of 1935, where the Rataul mango from our family orchard was declared the best mango in the world. Actively involved in the negotiations for Indian independence, Bapu would entertain extensively in the fortress and guest house. The family cooks would make milder dishes for the visiting English delegation, which later came to be known as Anglo-Indian cuisine (see Hussainy Curry on page 64). After partition and the independence of India and Pakistan, Bapu withdrew from politics and spent the remaining years of his life living a simple, spiritual life.

and raw. The damp, cold wind sliced through me. I remember running my hands along the rough, angry bark of a tree. I felt that the tree would never have a spring and that my life, too, was going to consist of unending days of unrelenting winter.

Then I learned to cook.

Ammu had taught me how to cook with patience, and this became my salvation when I returned to Cambridge from Calcutta. Whenever I cooked in my small college kitchen, I could feel the presence of my mother next to me. When I was young, my mother would always tell me to stand behind her when she cooked and not come close to the cooker. I was not particularly good at listening to instructions and would love to see inside the pot. My mother would then ask me to hold the edge of her *palu* (the end of the saree that is draped over the shoulder) and only then could I stay in the kitchen, a successful way of making sure I was behind her and away from the heat. Decades later, whenever I cooked and I touched any fabric in the kitchen, I was instantly taken back to my kitchen in India, holding the embroidered edge of Ammu's saree.

While I cooked, I would listen to old Rajesh Khanna songs and my father's favourite playback singer, Talat Mahmood. These songs were the soundtrack to my life, the life I had left behind. Now, they had become the soundtrack to which I cooked. I cooked the way you remember the lyrics of songs. If I heard a beat, I knew the rhythm immediately. I was cooking to heal. It was unhurried and the pace followed the lyrical voices of the singers my mother would listen to on the radio in Calcutta: Geeta Dutt, Rafi and Kishore Kumar.

I would describe how the food looked and tasted whenever I called Ammu. She would be so happy and tell me she was so impressed that I had such a good memory for the food. She will never know that I remembered her every word. I would stand barefoot in my Cambridge kitchen and walk on the stone tiles as it reminded me of the red cement floor of my Calcutta kitchen. Separated by oceans, I was still connected to Ammu every time I cooked – her saree fabric crushed between my fingers, immersed in the aromas of spices.

Top right: Ammu's favourite chocolate and me! This photo was taken in our small Cambridge studio flat. A few months later we moved to a much bigger flat in college so my husband could supervise his students in the study. Ammu would often hold or keep me close, as she is doing here. I missed that contact so much when she was not there.

Bottom right: Abbu hates being photographed and it always takes some convincing to get him to pose for a picture. And trying to get him to smile for a photograph is almost impossible!

# Ammu's Chicken Biryani

SERVES 6

Biryani was always made for big celebratory occasions. In my mother's family, it was usually made with *khasi*, or goat, and cooked in a giant pot with layers of rice, meat and potatoes infused with spices and saffron. This recipe is a very personal one. This was the biryani that was made just for the five of us – my parents, my two siblings and me. On days when there was some good news, or more typically on days when something had gone wrong – from my brother losing a cricket match or me not doing so well in my exams – Ammu would get this biryani on the table and suddenly everything seemed okay! This is also usually the last dish I eat at home before I make the five-hour car journey from my parents' home to the airport to catch my flight to London. I always felt that layered in that biryani were things my mother couldn't say. When the biryani arrived on the table, it felt like Ammu's secret code, telling me that she loved me.

## INGREDIENTS

200g plain flour

500g good-quality basmati rice

5 tbsp salt

½ tsp saffron strands

80ml full-fat milk

8 tbsp ghee or vegetable oil (sometimes I mix both and it works really well)

2 white onions, thinly sliced into half moons

1kg skinless chicken thighs, on the bone

3 garlic cloves, crushed

5–6-cm piece of fresh ginger, grated

2 tbsp full-fat Greek-style yoghurt

½ tsp chilli powder

2 green cardamom pods

2 cloves

1-cm piece of cinnamon stick

1-cm piece of mace, crushed

⅛ tsp grated nutmeg

¼ tsp sugar

juice of ½ lemon

## METHOD

Mix the flour with enough water to make a firm dough, cover and leave to rest.

Wash the rice in a bowl of cold water, moving your hand in gentle circular movements in one direction to avoid breaking the delicate tips of the rice (the virtually invisible tips, if broken off, will boil rapidly when the rice goes into the hot water, because of their size, and turn into glue-like starch, which will make all the rice sticky). Wash the rice in several changes of cold water until the water remains clear.

Next, soak the rice. There should be at least 15–20cm of water in the bowl above the rice level. Add 6 teaspoons of the salt and soak the rice for at least 2 hours. The long soaking allows the rice to absorb water. As the rice is not hollow and dry when it is put into boiling water, the cooking time is minimised; this will help keep your rice grains long and separate.

*Continues overleaf*

Put the saffron in a small bowl. Warm the milk to tepid: my mother would describe it as blood temperature – if you touch the milk it should feel only slightly warm. If you are using a microwave to heat the milk, remember to stir the milk before checking the temperature as there may be hot spots. Pour the tepid milk over the saffron and set aside to infuse.

Heat the ghee or oil in a heavy-based pan over a medium–high heat and fry the onions until caramelised. Using a slotted spoon and leaving as much of the oil in the pan as possible, remove the onions to a plate, spreading them across the plate to cool.

Remove half the oil from the pan and set aside. Add the chicken to the remaining oil and cook over a medium–high heat until golden brown on both sides. Add the garlic, ginger, yoghurt, chilli powder and 2 teaspoons of the salt and cook over a medium–high heat until the garlic and ginger have lost their raw smell and the yoghurt has reduced. Add half the caramelised onions, then add warm water to cover the chicken, bring to the boil, then cover and simmer for about 25 minutes. You do not want the chicken to be tender: it should still be firm, as it will be cooked further with the rice.

Drain the soaked rice. Boil the kettle and pour the water into a large pan. Bring back to the boil, add another 6 teaspoons salt, then add the drained rice and boil until the rice is three-quarters cooked (this should not take more than 5 minutes). To test, remove one grain from the boiling water and squeeze it. There should be a hard core to the grain of rice. When the rice reaches this stage, drain and spread it on a tray to prevent it from continuing to cook.

To assemble the biryani you will need a heavy-based pan with a tight-fitting lid. Using a slotted spoon, remove the chicken from its cooking liquid and place it in the pan. Strain the cooking liquid and pour over the chicken. Try to squeeze as much as you can from the onion/ginger/garlic residue, so the stock is nice and thick. It should just about cover the chicken pieces. Next, add the cardamom, cloves, cinnamon, mace and nutmeg. Add half the saffron milk, the sugar and squeezed lemon juice. Then add the rice, ensuring it covers the chicken. On top of the rice, add the remaining caramelised onions, the remaining saffron milk and the reserved oil.

Put the biryani pan over a high heat and wait until the steam starts coming out. Let the steam come through for 1 minute. Meanwhile, roll the dough into tubes and use the dough to seal the lid of the biryani pan. Put the pan on top of a cast-iron frying pan or *tawa* over a medium–high heat: this is to diffuse the heat. If you do not have a cast-iron pan, put the biryani pan into a preheated oven at 190°C/170°C fan/ gas 5 for 10 minutes. After 10 minutes, turn the oven to 150°C/130°C fan/gas 2 and leave for 20 minutes. If you are using a *tawa* on the hob, reduce the heat to low, cover the top of the pan with a folded clean kitchen cloth and leave for 20 minutes.

When ready to serve, unseal the biryani lid. Using a large spoon and starting from one side, gently lift the chicken up and mix with the rice. You need to gently merge the wet rice with the dry rice on the top, so each grain is perfectly moist.

Opposite, clockwise from top right:

Both of these pictures were taken in Calcutta. On the left, my nephew Farhan is photobombing a picture of us three siblings! On the right, sitting with my father, my mother is wearing her trademark chiffon printed saree.

I am standing under the gulmohar tree outside the *diwan* hall in the Chhatari fortress on a visit home.

A gathering of my mother's family. Standing are my grandparents, my grandfather's brothers and their wives. Sitting on the stairs is my mother in the middle with her cousins. My mother's uncles and aunts were great connoisseurs of food. Each aunt had a signature dish that was always the centrepiece of any party they hosted. The conversations were always about food while they ate, but the family had a reputation of not making any small talk after they had eaten. My grandfather would famously get up from the table to head straight for his car!

Ammu standing in a checked *kurta* with her sisters and my grandmother.

Me wearing a cardigan knitted by Ammu. I remember the colour was my favourite orangey red!

My maternal grandmother with a rifle. The 1940s were a turbulent time in our history, with the movement for independence and the bloody partition. My grandmother learned to use a gun for self-defence. She was raised in a home that had a great reputation for food. The breakfast at Bakhtiyarpur (her ancestral home in Bihar) was legendary. The *Baghare Aloo* on page 104 was part of it. Incredibly, of her five daughters, my mother and the youngest daughter, Allu Khala, were the only ones who could cook.

# Bharwan Kofta

## Stuffed Meat Kofta

This dish reminds me of my sister Amna. We often made this when she would visit with her children. She lived in Dhaka, Bangladesh, and this was a dish that was not made in that region. Sometimes, our cook Haji Saheb would make a special version for Amna with a chilli and onion stuffing

The ideal meat for this is mutton; it is not easily available, but if you can find it, please do use it. Beef with 10 per cent fat works really well, too. The cashew nut and raisin stuffing is a nice touch. You can substitute any other nut or dried fruit you may have in your kitchen cupboards, as long as it has a similar texture and does not release any liquid, which would make the kofta break up. Serve with plain boiled rice or *Channa Pulao* (page 272).

### INGREDIENTS

#### Kofta

2 slices of white bread, crusts removed

1kg finely minced beef or mutton

2 eggs

2 red onions, finely chopped

4 green chillies, chopped

1 tsp garam masala

¼ tsp grated nutmeg

1 tsp salt

vegetable oil, for frying and oiling

#### Stuffing

3 tbsp chopped raisins

3 tbsp chopped cashew nuts

#### Gravy

5 tbsp vegetable oil

2 dried red chillies

1 bay leaf

2 cloves

2 green cardamom pods

3 onions, blitzed to a paste in a food processor

3 tbsp ginger paste

2 tbsp garlic paste

3 tsp ground coriander

1 tsp ground turmeric

1 tsp salt

400ml water

4 tbsp tomato purée

2 tbsp ground almonds

400ml thick coconut milk

### METHOD

To make the kofta, soak the bread in cold water, then squeeze out all the liquid, break it into small lumps and place in a bowl. Add all the remaining kofta ingredients, apart from the oil, mix together and gently knead. Divide the mixture into 16 equal pieces and roll into balls, about 5cm in diameter.

Mix the raisins and cashews together and divide this stuffing mixture into 16 portions.

*Continues overleaf*

To stuff the kofta, oil your hands, as the meat may be sticky. Flatten a meatball in the palm of your hand. Add one portion of the stuffing and pinch the meat around the stuffing to form a ball again. Roll the meatball between your hands, ensuring there are no cracks so it does not open up during the cooking process.

Heat a little oil in a deep pan over a medium–high heat. Fry a few koftas at a time so the temperature of the oil does not fall too quickly. You just want to brown the outside of the koftas, but not to cook them. Drain the koftas and set aside.

To make the gravy, heat the oil in a deep pan over a medium–high heat. Add the dried chillies, bay leaf, cloves and cardamoms and stir for a few seconds until the spices and chillies darken. Remove with a slotted spoon, leaving as much of the oil in the pan as possible, and set aside on a plate. Keeping the heat at medium–high, add the onion paste – do not let this burn as it will give the gravy a bitter undertone, so add splashes of water to prevent the onion from burning. Once the raw aroma of the onion has reduced, which may take 4–5 minutes, add the ginger and garlic pastes and cook for 5 minutes. Add the coriander, turmeric and salt to the pan, then cook, stirring, for 2 minutes.

Add the water, increase the heat to high and bring to the boil. Add the tomato purée, the fried chillies, bay leaf, cloves and cardamom and stir until the gravy is smooth.

Add the fried koftas to the pan and try to spread them out so they are almost submerged in the gravy. Bring to the boil, reduce the heat, cover and simmer for 20 minutes.

Remove the lid, add the ground almonds and bring the gravy to a rolling boil for 10 minutes until all the excess moisture has evaporated and the oil has come to the surface. Add the coconut milk and cook, stirring, for a further 5 minutes.

Taste and adjust the seasoning before serving.

Top: Ammu and me in Holland Park. Ammu wears a saree so elegantly. I inherited the cooking genes, but sadly not the elegance genes!

Middle left: Our family in our Bright Street flat in Calcutta. It was most likely Eid, as both Abbu and Arif are wearing traditional *kurta* pyjamas. My sons would never agree to wear these for Eid, but they did for the first time when I was writing this book.

Middle right: My parents in the courtyard of their home – the scene of many a family feast. Ammu is wearing her usual *shalwar kameez* and *dupatta* (scarf) in her favourite shade of blue.

Bottom: Rawdon Street was my mother's home in Calcutta and this is the room in which she was born. When my maternal grandfather passed away, the five sisters asked their children to gather at the home to celebrate his life. On the bed is Ammu, her four sisters, Amna, my cousins, an aunt and me. The power of a female collective is something I learned about from a very young age!

# Bhuna Khichuri

## Bengali Roasted Moong Dal and Rice

SERVES 6–8 (OR HALVE THE QUANTITIES IF YOU ARE MAKING IT FOR FEWER PEOPLE)

This is probably my favourite rice and lentil dish. It is a deeply comforting and nourishing recipe. I often make it when I want something healing and if I have homemade ghee to hand I add a dollop of it on top of the rice. I always feel better after I eat this *khichuri*!

There were various versions of this dish made in my family, but there was only one version I really disliked, the one that was made when someone was ill. It was almost like a medicine, as it was made with masoor dal, which breaks down more easily and is easy to digest. The 'medicinal' version was watery and bland – rice and lentils were simply boiled together until they became total mush, with the consistency of thick soup. Unfortunately, even if you were not ill you had to eat the same food as your siblings, as no one was going to cook anything special for you. I thought that was so unfair – not only did you have to go to school, as you were not sick, but when you came home you had to eat the bland rice and lentil dish. *Bhuna khichuri* was completely different. Cooked with a lot more care, it had a wonderful smoky, earthy fragrance as the lentils were dry-roasted before cooking. The roasted dal does not break down and keeps its shape. It is garnished with the fried onions.

We would eat this year-round, but my memory is of us eating this rice dish during the late monsoons, which was always malaria season and invariably a time when many people became unwell. This was usually served in my house with a couple of accompanying *bhortas*, such as the Tomato Bhorta on page 218.

### INGREDIENTS

200g moong dal

400g basmati rice

200ml vegetable oil or ghee

300g white onion, thinly sliced into half moons

3 green cardamom pods

2 x 2.5-cm pieces of cassia bark

2 Indian bay leaves (*tej patta*)

1½ tsp ground turmeric

1 litre warm water

2½ tsp salt

5-cm piece of fresh ginger, grated

6 whole green chillies

### METHOD

In a dry *karai* or wok, dry roast the moong dal over a medium heat. My mother insists the dal should always be roasted in a cast-iron pan or *karai* – any pan with a thick base will ensure that the dal does not burn. You need the heat of the pan to be evenly distributed and diffused. The dal should slowly darken and start to emit a beautiful earthy, smoky fragrance. Keep stirring the dal to ensure that all the grains are roasted evenly. Turn the roasted dal onto a large plate and leave to cool.

*Continues overleaf*

Very gently wash the rice and cooled dal in a bowl of cold water. Change the water several times until it is no longer cloudy. Leave the dal and rice to soak in cold water while you prepare the onions.

Heat the oil or ghee in a large pan over a medium heat and fry the onions until they are caramelised. Using a slotted spoon, remove the onions to a plate, leaving as much of the oil in the pan as possible. Separate the onions with a fork and spread across the plate so they crisp as they cool (do not use kitchen paper).

Drain the dal and rice from the water and spread them on kitchen paper. Gently pat them dry with more kitchen paper.

Put the pan with the oil or ghee back over a medium heat. Add the cardamoms, cassia bark and bay leaves and then the drained dal and rice. Add the turmeric and gently stir to coat the dal and rice with the oil and spices. Add the warm water and salt and bring to the boil, then cover with a lid and simmer for at least 20–30 minutes, stirring regularly, until all the water has been absorbed.

Add the grated ginger and green chillies and gently mix through the rice and lentils. Put the lid back on and turn off the heat. Leave the pan on the hob, covered with a clean kitchen cloth, for about another 30 minutes before serving. Garnish with the caramelised onions.

Above right: Ammu and me at Amna's home in Dhaka. Ammu would always come to Dhaka when I flew there to visit my mother-in-law. It was like our Bright Street days again. We would huddle together and chat and Amna's boys would come and go. Our conversations continued deep into the night.

Right: Cambridge, 1992, with Arif, Ammu and Abbu along the River Cam. My family stayed in college and I could see Ammu realising how this was so different to Calcutta. When they were leaving, it was first time I saw my mother cry when she said goodbye. It has been 30 years since I left home and I still weep when I say goodbye to Ammu.

# Hara Korma

## Lamb Shanks in Yoghurt and Herb Gravy

SERVES 6–8

This is a great dish to make if you are new to Indian cooking or wary of 'ruining' expensive meat by overcooking it. The worst that can happen is that some of the meat may start to fall off the bone when you serve it, and that is not a disaster at all. In this way, it's also easy to test whether the dish is cooked perfectly – just pull some meat off from the top or bottom of the shank to check.

If you are more used to cooking for one or two people, scaling up can sometimes feel intimidating, but this is a good dish to make for a party. The challenge can be finding a large enough pan to cook greater quantities of meat, but you can cook this in two pans if necessary. Do keep in mind that this is a sharing dish so there is unlikely to be one shank per person. Sometimes, it helps if you 'carve' the meat by pulling it loose from the bone before serving your guests. Serve with a rice pulao.

### INGREDIENTS

200ml vegetable oil

8 white onions, thinly sliced into half moons

50g whole raw cashews

50g whole raw almonds

5–6-cm piece of fresh ginger, grated

4 garlic cloves, crushed

2 tbsp ground coriander

2 large handfuls of fresh coriander (leaves and stalks)

1 large handful of fresh mint leaves (no stalks)

4 green chillies

1kg full-fat Greek-style yoghurt

2 x 2.5-cm pieces of cassia bark

2 large Indian bay leaves (*tej patta*)

6 green cardamom pods

2kg lamb shanks

1 tsp salt

juice of 1 lime

1½ tsp sugar

100ml thick or double cream

### METHOD

Heat the oil in a large, deep casserole dish or pan with a lid over a medium–high heat for about 5 minutes. Take a slice of onion and dip the tip into the oil – it should start to sizzle immediately. If not, heat the oil for a bit longer and check again. Add all the onions to the pan and do not stir for the first few minutes as that will lower the temperature of the oil. After 2 minutes, you can start to stir the onions to ensure they are cooking evenly. Slowly fry for about 20 minutes until brown and caramelised. Using a slotted spoon and leaving as much of the oil in the pan as possible, remove the onions to a plate, spreading them across the plate to cool.

Reduce the heat to low, add the cashews to the pan and stir until they turn a few shades darker. Remove the cashews with a slotted spoon and place on top of the fried onions.

*Continues overleaf*

Next, add the almonds to the pan (you may need to increase the heat if there are no bubbles or sizzling sound) and fry briefly to remove the rawness – it is important not to burn the almonds. Remove the almonds with a slotted spoon and add to the onions and cashews. Keep the pan and oil for later.

Transfer the onions and nuts to a grinder and grind together to make a paste. Add the ginger, garlic and ground coriander and grind until incorporated. Chop the fresh coriander with the stalks, mint leaves and chillies, then add them to the grinder along with 1 tablespoon of water. Grind until the mixture is smooth. Transfer the green paste to a bowl and mix with the yoghurt.

Reheat the oil in the pan over a medium–high heat. Add the cassia bark, bay leaves and cardamoms and fry briefly, then remove with a slotted spoon. Add the lamb shanks to the pan, one at a time, and fry until browned all over. As each one is browned, remove from the pan and set aside. Once all the shanks have been browned, return them to the pan and pour over the green yoghurt mixture, followed by the salt, and the fried cassia bark, cardamoms and bay leaves. Bring to the boil, then reduce the heat, cover and cook slowly for about 2 hours.

When the meat is cooked (see introduction), add the lime juice and sugar, stir, then taste and adjust the seasoning. Increase the heat and cook to reduce any excess liquid – you want a thick sauce that clings to the meat. When you are ready to serve, pour the cream over the top.

*Tip*

The lamb shanks can be replaced with poussin, diced lamb shoulder, spring lamb leg or beef short ribs. The meat will need to be browned before cooking and the cooking time adjusted to suit the meat you are using.

Top: Ammu in New Market in Calcutta, in the haberdashery shop. I would take all my torn outfits or things to be altered back to Calcutta and my mother would repair all my clothes! She was incredibly skilled and would stitch in almost an invisible way. You could never see the tear had been repaired.

Above: This picture was taken on my last trip to Ammu's ancestral home in Calcutta. The home where she was born and where I was the last grandchild to walk down the beautiful wooden stairs as a bride. My mother's cousin, Azmat Bhaiya, who was visiting, suggested a final celebration before I left and arranged all the ingredients for me to cook. For the first time, I was cooking for my family in a space where I had eaten endless meals as a child. The memory of that meal is poingant as we sadly lost Azmat Bhaiya to Covid in 2020. I decided to cook Calcutta Haka food (see the recipes on page 260 and 262), as I was too intimidated to cook my family recipes in our ancestral home! My aunt Farhat Khala, who cannot cook at all, offered to be my assistant, together with Ammu. Luckily, everything turned out really well and I could see my mother beaming with pride at the end of the meal.

# Eid ka Murgh Kabab

## Chicken Kabab

SERVES 6–8

Unlike a dinner party, when all the guests arrived at the same time, on Eid visitors would drop in all day and the food had to be constantly replenished as new guests arrived. The chicken kabab was marinated the night before and skewered on thin metal sticks or *seekhs* in the morning, ready to be cooked when required. This kabab can be grilled indoors or cooked on a barbecue. The chicken can also be cooked without skewers – spread it on a foil-covered baking tin and cook under a preheated medium grill. This is really good with *Saag ka Raita* (page 50) and *Khaas Aloo* (page 208).

### INGREDIENTS

1kg boneless, skinless chicken thighs, cut into 5-cm pieces

200g full-fat Greek-style yoghurt

2 tbsp fresh lime juice

8 garlic cloves, finely chopped

1 large white onion, sliced

5-cm piece of fresh ginger, grated

1 tsp salt

½ tsp chilli powder

1 tsp sugar

4 tbsp ghee

1 tsp rose water

lemon wedges, to serve

### METHOD

Put the chicken in a bowl, add all the remaining ingredients and mix well. Marinate in a covered container overnight in the fridge.

Let the chicken come to room temperature before cooking.

Preheat the grill to medium and skewer the chicken. Do not pack the skewers tightly as this will prevent the chicken from cooking evenly. Cook for 7–10 minutes, turning the skewers frequently.

Serve hot, with lemon wedges.

# Gobi Masala

## Spiced Cauliflower

Cauliflower season in Bengal was in the cooler months. The cauliflower would arrive at home from the bazaar piled high on a rickshaw. The arrival of *gobi masala* on the table was the first sign that the season had begun. I loved the season for another reason, too, as it was the time when the traditional potato *shingara* (Bengali samosas stuffed with potatoes and cauliflowers) would also be served – another dish I adored.

This cauliflower dish can be served with bread or rice. The cauliflower florets are cut with 'long tails' and cooked using minimum liquid, so that the cauliflower becomes tender without losing its shape. Serve with rotis and an accompanying chutney, such as *Lal Chutney* (page 34).

### INGREDIENTS

2 tbsp vegetable oil

3 tbsp ghee

1 tsp cumin seeds

2 dried red chillies, broken

1kg cauliflower, cut into small florets with long stems

½ tsp ground turmeric

2.5-cm piece of fresh ginger, grated

1½ tsp salt

1 tbsp fresh lemon juice

2 tbsp full-fat Greek-style yoghurt

fresh coriander, to garnish (optional)

### METHOD

You will need a deep frying pan with a tight-fitting lid. Heat the oil and ghee over a medium–high heat, then add the cumin seeds and dried chillies, followed by the cauliflower florets. Stir-fry for a minute and then reduce the heat, cover with the lid and leave for 2 minutes. *Remove the lid, increase the heat and stir-fry the cauliflower for another minute. Reduce the heat again, cover with the lid and leave for 2 minutes. Repeat this process from the * once more.

Remove the lid, add the turmeric, ginger, salt, lemon juice and yoghurt and stir-fry over a high heat for a minute. Reduce the heat, cover the pan and leave for 2 minutes. Stir-fry over a high heat and then reduce the heat and cook, covered, for 2 more minutes. Finally, stir-fry for a minute or so until all the liquid has reduced.

Serve hot, garnished with coriander, if you like.

# Prawn Biryani

A prawn biryani is a great alternative to a traditional meat-based biryani, and instead of prawns you can substitute pieces of firm, white fish, such as cod, or even salmon. The preparation is in two parts. First, you need to make a spiced prawn base, which is layered with rice, saffron and spices, and then the rice and prawns are gently cooked together to merge the flavours. As with all seafood dishes, the most important thing is not to overcook the prawns.

## INGREDIENTS

700g basmati rice

7 tsp salt

1 Indian bay leaf (*tej patta*) or regular bay leaf

4 green cardamom pods

2 cloves

5-cm piece of cassia bark (or cinnamon stick)

1 tbsp ghee

*Saffron Layer*

1 tsp saffron strands

100ml full-fat milk

*Prawn Layer*

4 tbsp vegetable oil

100g white onion, thinly sliced

½ tsp sugar

4 tbsp ghee

175g onions, blitzed to a paste in a food processor

1 tbsp ginger paste

1 tsp garlic paste

½ tsp ground turmeric

1 tsp ground cumin

1 tsp ground coriander

1 tsp chilli powder

3 small red tomatoes, chopped

1 tsp salt

500g raw peeled prawns, deveined

## METHOD

Wash the rice in a bowl of cold water, moving your hand in gentle circular movements in one direction to avoid breaking the delicate tips of the rice (if they are broken they will form a glue-like starch that will make the rice sticky). Change the water several times until it is no longer cloudy. Soak the rice in cold water for 1–3 hours.

Put the saffron in a small bowl, warm the milk to tepid and pour over the saffron. Set aside.

To make the prawn layer, heat the oil in a heavy-based pan over a medium–high heat. To check that the oil is hot enough, take a slice of onion and dip the tip into the oil – it should immediately start to sizzle. If not, wait for a few more minutes before adding all the sliced onion. Sprinkle the sugar over the onion and fry for 15–20 minutes or until caramelised. As the onion starts to turn golden brown, keep stirring to ensure it fries evenly. Using a slotted spoon, remove the onion to a plate, leaving as much of the oil in the pan as possible. Separate the onion with a fork and spread across the plate so it crisps as it cools.

*Continued overleaf*

Put the pan back over a medium–high heat and add the ghee, quickly followed by the onion paste, ginger and garlic pastes and stir for 2–3 minutes. Add the turmeric, cumin, coriander and chilli powder and stir for a minute. Add the tomatoes and salt and pour about 2cm of water over the contents of the pan, then cook until the liquid starts to reduce and thicken, and you can see oil at the edges of the tomato mixture. Add the prawns and cook over a high heat for 2–5 minutes, stirring to ensure all the prawns are cooked, but taking care not to overcook them. Remove the pan from the heat and set aside, uncovered. There should be a thick clingy sauce around the prawns.

Use a large pan to boil the rice. Boil the kettle and fill the pan up to three-quarters of its depth with boiling water. Drain the rice and add to the boiling water together with the 7 teaspoons of salt, bay leaf, cardamoms, cloves and cassia. Boil the rice until it is three-quarters cooked (this should not take more than 5 minutes). This is important as it will go through another cooking process. To test, remove one grain of rice from the boiling water and press it between your fingers. The outside should be soft but there should still be a hard inner core in the grain of rice. When the rice reaches this stage, drain in a colander and then spread the rice out on a couple of large plates to prevent it from continuing to cook.

To assemble the biryani you will need a heavy-based pan with a tight-fitting lid. First add half the rice. Add ½ teaspoon of the ghee and half the saffron milk and stir gently to ensure the ghee and milk spread evenly. Then add the prawn mixture, including any sauce. Sprinkle a quarter of the caramelised onions on top of the prawn layer followed by the remaining rice. Add the remaining saffron milk and the remaining ghee. Sprinkle another quarter of the caramelised onions on top. Put the pan over a high heat and wait until you can see some steam coming through from more than one area. When the steam is coming through evenly, cover the pan tightly and turn the heat to low. After 15 minutes, turn off the heat and leave undisturbed for 10 minutes.

Remove the lid and gently mix the layers. Garnish with the remaining onions before serving.

Opposite top and below left: The humanities class of 1987, La Martiniere school, Calcutta. I studied history, politics, English and sociology. I am the curly haired girl in the middle of the second row. When we left school, many of my classmates left to study in the US and I lost touch with them. All I had was this picture and their signatures. Decades later, we all reconnected via the internet. Many of the Anglo-Indian dishes I got to know were through my school friends, such as the *Hussainy Curry* on page 64.

Middle right: My mother would love to make me wear her sarees. This was my last visit to my Calcutta home before my parents moved to Aligarh. That house held so many memories and I still miss it.

Bottom: A relaxed Phopoo Jani in my London home. My aunt had got a few days off from hospital and we had invited her to our home. I was still unable to cook, so the dinner that night was cooked by Mushtaq. The next day, my aunt called my mother and told her she was going to teach me some basic dishes when we returned to Cambridge!

# Pot-Roast Beef

SERVES 6 (WITH LEFTOVERS)

I only realised the strong British influence on Calcutta's cuisine when I moved to England. Most Indian homes do not have ovens, so this is a great pot-roasted beef to make the most of a cut of meat that would be cooked on the hob. In India, we would use 'undercut', a cheap cut of beef that responds well to long, slow cooking. Serve hot with rotis, like the *Zaffran Rogni Roti* (page 224) or *Khamiri Roti* (page 162).

I loved the sandwiches that were made from the leftovers of the roast beef. The next day, we would thinly slice the beef and sandwich it between white bread with a thick layer of butter and have tomato ketchup on the side.

### INGREDIENTS

2kg beef brisket

250g full-fat Greek-style yoghurt

2 tbsp ginger paste

1 tbsp garlic paste

120ml malt vinegar

3 tsp salt

120ml vegetable oil

2 litres boiling water

2 tsp black peppercorns

sliced red onions, to garnish

### METHOD

Use a fork to prick the beef all over. Mix the yoghurt, ginger, garlic, vinegar and salt in a large bowl, add the beef and marinate overnight.

Let the meat come to room temperature before cooking: this may take as long as 3 hours.

Lift the beef out of the marinade, scraping the marinade back into the bowl, and use kitchen paper to wipe off the marinade from the meat. Heat the oil in a heavy-based pan over a medium–high heat. Add the meat and brown it all over.

Add the marinade to the pan a little at a time. Once you've added all the marinade, pour in the boiling water and peppercorns and bring back to the boil. Reduce the heat, cover the pan and simmer for about 4 hours until the meat is tender.

Remove the lid and simmer so the gravy reduces and thickens.

Garnish with sliced red onions and serve.

# Methi Chicken

## Chicken with Fenugreek

The earthy flavour of *kasur methi* (dried fenugreek) gives this dish its distinctive taste. The base is a rich combination of yoghurt and tomato. The beautiful orange-red gravy goes really well with a rice pulao, such as *Sada Pulao* (page 198) or *Channa Pulao* (page 272). It is a great dish to cook when entertaining if there is no room to seat a lot of people, as the boneless chicken makes it easy for people to stand to eat and not need to use a knife. When my mother wanted to be a bit more indulgent, she would add a big dollop of white unsalted butter and a drizzle of thick cream. Feel free to add that extra touch to this dish.

### INGREDIENTS

4 tbsp vegetable oil

2 onions, thinly sliced into half moons

2.5-cm piece of cassia bark

2 green cardamom pods

1 clove

1 Indian bay leaf (*tej patta*)

2 dried red chillies

1kg boneless skinless chicken thighs

5–6-cm piece of fresh ginger, grated

3 garlic cloves, crushed

1 tsp ground turmeric

1 tbsp ground coriander

200g full-fat Greek-style yoghurt

1 tsp dried fenugreek leaves (*kasur methi*)

1 tsp each salt and chilli powder

4 tbsp tomato purée

½ tsp sugar

### SERVES 6

*To Garnish (optional)*

4 tbsp double cream (do add if you can!)

handful of fresh coriander leaves

### METHOD

Heat the oil in a heavy-based pan over a medium–high heat. Add the onions and fry, stirring occasionally, for about 20 minutes until golden brown and caramelised. Use a slotted spoon to remove the onions, leaving as much of the oil in the pan as possible, and place on a plate to drain. Spread the onions across the plate so they crisp as they cool.

Add the cassia bark, cardamoms, clove, bay leaf and red chillies to the pan, then add the chicken and cook over a medium–high heat until golden brown all over.

Reduce the heat to medium, add the ginger and garlic and stir for about 2 minutes until the garlic no longer smells raw. Add the turmeric and ground coriander and stir for a minute, then add the yoghurt, followed by the fenugreek leaves. Do not let the yoghurt boil – you should not need to add any water, as the yoghurt will prevent the spices from sticking to the base of the pan. Add the caramelised onions, salt, chilli powder and tomato purée and stir gently. Reduce the heat, cover and simmer for 5 minutes.

Remove the lid, stir in the sugar until it has dissolved, then taste and adjust the seasoning. Increase the heat to medium–high and stir, uncovered, until the oil comes to the surface.

Serve hot, garnished with cream and coriander, if using.

# Saag Channa Masala

## Spinach with Chickpeas

SERVES 4–6

This was one of the meatless dishes we ate on Thursdays. Once a week, the meat market in Calcutta was closed and households that usually ate meat would eat vegetarian food. Many years later, I read an article promoting Meat-free Monday in England and I realised that many people had been doing this in India for years! It makes sense to reduce our consumption of meat, and looking at ways to support the environment by adapting our food choices is a good idea. Serve with *Gobi Masala* (page 144) and *Dosti Roti* (page 60).

### INGREDIENTS

350g dried white chickpeas

3 dried red chillies

1 tsp cumin seeds

6 tbsp vegetable oil

200g onions, sliced

6 garlic cloves, crushed

2 tbsp grated fresh ginger

1 tbsp ground coriander

1 tsp chilli powder

4 tbsp tomato purée

500ml warm water

1 tsp salt

1 spicy green chilli, cut in half

½ tsp garam masala

2 tsp *amchur* (dried mango powder)

500g baby spinach, washed

### METHOD

Wash the chickpeas in cold running water in a colander, then put them in a large bowl, cover with cold water and leave to soak for at least 6 hours or preferably overnight. The chickpeas will double in volume so ensure you use a suitable bowl and add at least 1.5 litres water.

Drain the chickpeas and put them in a pan, cover with fresh water and bring to the boil. Add the dried red chillies, cover and simmer for 30–40 minutes until the chickpeas are cooked. Drain and set aside with the red chillies.

Meanwhile, dry roast the cumin seeds in a heavy-based pan over a low heat, stirring until they turn a few shades darker. Tip them onto a plate and leave to cool. Grind to a powder, using a spice grinder or a pestle and mortar.

Heat the oil in a deep pan over a medium–high heat. Add the onions and fry for 15 minutes until they turn a rich brown colour. Add the garlic and ginger and stir for a minute. Then add the ground roasted cumin, coriander and chilli powder, followed by the tomato purée. Add the warm water and return the chickpeas and red chillies to the pan with the salt. Keep the liquid at a slow rolling boil until it has reduced to a thick clingy sauce around the chickpeas.

Add the green chilli, garam masala and *amchur* and continue to cook until the oil comes to the surface and the chickpeas are glistening. Finally, add the spinach and stir through. Turn off the heat. Taste and adjust the seasoning, then serve.

# Lahsun Mirch Chutney

## Garlic and Chilli Chutney

A robust garlic and chilli chutney, which goes well with all meals. The heat of this chutney can be reduced by using milder, larger fresh chillies. The rule to remember is that the smaller the chilli, the more fiery it will be. A good compromise would be to mix larger and smaller chillies, as you need some larger chillies to provide body to the chutney.

There is another version of this chutney which is very spicy: it uses 20 dried red chillies, which you soak in hot water for an hour; you then remove the stalks and grind to a paste in the same way as for the fresh chillies.

### INGREDIENTS

20 fresh red chillies

12–16 garlic cloves

2 tbsp fresh lime juice

1 tbsp vegetable oil

1 tsp salt

### METHOD

If there are any stems on the chillies, break them off carefully to ensure the chillies stay intact.

Put the chillies and garlic in a blender or spice grinder and grind, adding 1–2 tablespoons of water to make a smooth paste. Add the lime juice, oil and salt and mix well.

Leave for 4 hours to mature before eating.

You can keep the chutney in a sealed container in the fridge for a couple of days, but a word of warning: the heat will increase as the chillies infuse further.

# Kancha Aamer Chutney

## Raw Mango Chutney

SERVES 6

Home-made chutney may seem like a luxury, but this chutney is definitely worth the effort. Infused with *panch phoran*, the Bengali five-seed spice mix, this chutney has so many childhood memories attached to it. You can replace the raisins with other dried fruit, such as apricots or cranberries. Raw green mangoes are available in most Asian shops around the year. If you are unable to find raw mangoes, you can make this chutney with the really hard unripe mangoes you can get in some supermarkets.

Serve with *Sada Pulao* (page 198) and *Hariyali Murgh* (page 98).

### INGREDIENTS

5 raw mangoes

salt, to taste

1 tbsp vegetable oil

¼ tsp panch phoran

2 dried red chillies

120ml water

½ tbsp raisins

500g sugar

### METHOD

Peel and slice the mangoes, sprinkle with some salt and set aside for 1 hour.

After an hour, pat the mangoes with kitchen paper until thoroughly dry.

Heat the oil in a pan over a medium heat, add the panch phoran and dried chillies, followed by the mango slices, and fry for a few minutes. Add the water and raisins and half the sugar. Taste before adding more sugar as the sourness of raw mango can vary a lot.

Add ½ teaspoon of salt and cook on a low simmer until the mango softens. You may need to add more salt or sugar as it cooks down. Taste and adjust the seasoning and sweetness before you turn off the heat.

This chutney does not have a long shelf life and needs to be kept covered in the fridge, for up to a week.

# Kala Channa

## Black Chickpeas

Black chickpeas have a wonderful nutty flavour. More dense than white chickpeas, they're packed with protein and soluble fibre. In the eastern Indian state of Bihar, they are a popular source of nourishment for daily wagers who work long, gruelling hours. In many households observing Ramadan, they are often eaten at sunset when the fast ends. *Kala Channa* has strong memories of Ramadan for me. My first Ramadan after leaving India was in Cambridge; I went to the Pakistani store to ask if they had this chickpea. They didn't, but the shopkeeper told me to wait and came back with two pomegranates from the back of his shop and gave them to me. He said nothing. He did not need to. He probably saw the disappointment in my eyes and wanted to give me something. He came out to watch me cycle away and waved until he could no longer see me.

### INGREDIENTS

240g dried black chickpeas

2 dried red chillies

1 tsp cumin seeds

4 tbsp vegetable oil

120g white onion, thinly sliced

6 garlic cloves, crushed

2 tbsp grated fresh ginger

1 green chilli, cut in half

1 tbsp ground coriander

1 tsp chilli powder

2 tbsp tomato purée

1½ tbsp salt

½ tsp garam masala

SERVES 4

### METHOD

Wash the chickpeas under cold running water. Put them in a large bowl, cover with cold water and leave to soak for at least 6 hours or preferably overnight. The chickpeas will double in volume so ensure you use a suitable bowl and add at least 1.5 litres water.

Drain the chickpeas and put them in a pan, cover with fresh water and bring to the boil. Add the dried red chillies, cover and simmer for 1–1½ hours. Check after 1 hour – the chickpeas should be firm but soft inside (the outside will not soften). If the inside is still hard, continue to simmer until the chickpeas have a creamy consistency inside. Drain and set aside.

Meanwhile, dry roast the cumin seeds in a heavy-based pan over a low heat, stirring until they turn a few shades darker. Tip them onto a plate and leave to cool. Grind to a powder, using a spice grinder or a pestle and mortar.

Heat the oil in a deep pan over a medium–high heat. Add the onion and fry for about 15 minutes until rich and brown. Add the garlic, ginger and green chilli and stir for a minute, then add the ground roasted cumin, coriander and chilli powder, followed by the tomato purée. Add 500ml warm water and return the chickpeas and red chillies to the pan with the salt. Keep the liquid at a slow rolling boil until it has reduced to a thick clingy sauce. Add the garam masala and continue to cook until the oil comes to the surface and the chickpeas are glistening. Taste and adjust the seasoning before serving with *Khamiri Roti* (page 162) or, if you prefer, *Saag ka Raita* (page 50).

# Khamiri Roti

## Mughlai Roti

SERVES 6 (MAKES 12 ROTIS)

Ammu would always ensure that we would have roti at every dinner, as my father grew up in a wheat-growing area and rice was only served for big family celebrations. I heard a story of my mother's first meal in my father's ancestral home, where *khamiri roti* was served for lunch. My mother, who grew up eating rice rather than bread, ate the roti by breaking pieces of it, placing the accompanying food onto the roti and then rolling it up like a wrap, which amused all of my father's relatives. The traditional way to eat roti is to use pieces of it to scoop up the food. Ironically, Ammu's style of eating was taken up by me and my siblings, but whenever I watch people eating this way I remember how awkward my mother must have felt and how alienated, sitting at a table with food with which she was unfamiliar.

This is a very simple bread to make and is a great accompaniment to any Indian meal. It is also good to use as a wrap and take on a picnic. Unlike chapati, which harden when they cool, *khamiri roti*, if wrapped carefully in paper or foil, will stay soft and can be refrigerated for up to 2 days. I reheat them in a non-stick dry frying pan.

### INGREDIENTS

250g plain flour, plus extra for dusting

2 tsp fast-action dried yeast

1 tsp sugar

½ tsp salt

about 120ml lukewarm milk

60ml lukewarm water

4 tbsp ghee

### METHOD

Mix the flour with the yeast, sugar and salt and gradually add the milk and water to make a firm dough. Knead on a lightly floured surface for 5–6 minutes. Rub with half the ghee, cover and set aside in a warm place for an hour.

Put the dough on a floured surface, then knock back and knead the dough to remove all the air. Divide the dough into 12 pieces, shape each piece into a ball and roll out each ball to a 15-cm circle.

Put a *tawa* or frying pan over a medium–high heat. Cook one roti at a time, pressing the edges down to ensure it cooks evenly. When the bread puffs up, turn and cook on the other side. Brush a thin layer of ghee on the hot roti and serve.

*Pictured with Shami Kabab (page 110).*

# Nimki

## Crispy Nigella Seed Snacks

SERVES 4–6

Before mass-produced western-inspired snacks hit the shops (which happened a few years after I left India), a snack like *nimki* – or regional variations of deep-fried spiced dough, such as *namak para* and *mathri* – was what most of us would eat with tea. *Nimki* can be stored in an airtight container and kept for a few weeks. In my house it barely lasted a day. We rarely made this at home and would buy it from a roadside stall; my favourite was the *chanachur wallah* (snack vendor) in Park Circus market, who had a bewildering collection of fried snacks in glass jars and display cabinets. If anyone asked him if the item they were buying was fresh, his standard reply was '*Abhi bana*', 'I just made it.' I was never quite sure when the *nimki* was made, but I absolutely loved it! He would carefully measure out 500g on the scale, pouring one *nimki* at a time into the paper bag. If the scale went over, he would always take it out. If you paid for 500g of *nimki*, that was exactly how much you were going to get!

### INGREDIENTS

250g plain flour, plus extra for dusting

⅛ tsp baking powder

1 tsp kalonji (nigella seeds)

1½ tsp salt

3 tbsp melted unsalted butter or ghee

6 tbsp cold water

vegetable oil, for frying

### METHOD

Sift the flour with the baking powder into a bowl. Add the nigella seeds, salt and the melted butter or ghee and crumble into small lumps. Add the water a little at a time to make a firm but pliable dough. Alternatively, you can make the dough in a food processor. Cover the dough and set aside for 30 minutes.

Divide the dough into four pieces (this makes it more manageable). Roll out to about 5mm thick. Using a knife, cut the dough into strips about 4cm long and 1cm wide. You could also cut them into similar-sized diamond shapes, but they should all be the same size and shape so they cook at the same rate.

Meanwhile, heat a 6cm depth of oil in a *karai* or wok over a high heat. Reduce the heat to low and fry the *nimki* in small batches until golden brown. As the *nimki* are done, remove them using a slotted spoon and spread out on a non-metallic plate to cool completely and become crisp, before transferring to an airtight container, where they should keep for up to 2 weeks.

# Badam Barfi

## Almond Fudge

In this recipe, I have given precise quantities, but when my mother was teaching me to cook, there was always an element of *andaaz* or 'estimate'. My mother would say 'add a pinch', 'a touch of that – and a bit more' and then look at me as if I was out of my mind when I dared to ask what she meant. I have since discovered that this 'mum' style of teaching transcends borders. When my Singaporean friend was learning to make noodles, and my American PA was trying to learn how to make fried chicken, they both had similar experiences of vague verbal instructions from their mothers. I have now worked out the proportions and there is no *andaaz* here, so please be assured that you will end up with a proper fudge! This will keep in the fridge for 3 days.

### INGREDIENTS

225g shelled almonds

450g granulated sugar

flaked almonds or dried rose petals, to decorate (optional)

### METHOD

Put the almonds into a large bowl, pour over boiling water to cover and leave to soak for 10 minutes. Drain the nuts and then pour over more boiling water and leave to soak for a further 10 minutes. Drain again and when the nuts are cool enough to handle, rub them with a clean cloth to remove the skins. Put the skinless nuts back in the bowl, add cold water to cover and leave to soak for 1 hour. Check that they are soft: you may need to soak them for a bit longer (another hour or so) if they are still slightly hard. When soft, drain the nuts and whizz in a blender with about 100ml fresh cold water to make a smooth paste.

Transfer the paste to a heavy-based pan and cook over a medium heat for 10–12 minutes. Reduce the heat if the almond paste looks as though it may stick.

Line a 20-cm square cake tin with greased baking paper.

Meanwhile, put the sugar in another pan and add 125ml water. Place over a low heat, stirring occasionally until the sugar has dissolved. Bring the syrup to the boil over a medium heat. When it is boiling, add it to the almond paste. Gently mix the sugar and almond paste together and cook over a low–medium heat for 15–20 minutes. The mixture will spit, so be careful. The aim is to remove most of the moisture from the mixture, but keep your eye on it, as the consistency can quickly change from creamy and soft to crystallised. When the mixture is coming away from the sides of the pan and almost forming a ball, pour it into the lined tin. The almond paste should be around 1.5cm deep. Use a damp palette knife to level and smooth the surface.

Leave in a cool place for about 1 hour, until the mixture looks half-set, then cut into diamond shapes using a wet, sharp knife. Wipe the blade after each cut and wet it again for a clean cut. If using, place a flaked almond or a rose petal on each diamond shape. Cover and place in the fridge to harden, preferably overnight.

# Zarda

## Sweet Rice with Saffron and Nuts

SERVES 4–6

Anyone attending a *milad* (religious gathering) or a Muslim wedding in the subcontinent would have come across this saffron-infused glistening dessert. Saffron is one of the world's most expensive spices, but you only need a little, and infusing it in warm milk is a very effective way to bring out its flavour. The addition of nuts gives this dessert a further luxurious touch. Definitely serve with some thick or clotted cream on the side.

### INGREDIENTS

½ tsp saffron strands

2 tbsp full-fat milk

250g basmati rice

100g ghee or butter (or flavourless vegetable oil), plus extra for greasing

6 cloves

8 green cardamom pods

40g each shelled unsalted pistachios and unsalted blanched almonds, cut into thick slivers

30g dried apricots, cut into small cubes

150g granulated sugar

2 tbsp kewra (screwpine) water or rose water

### METHOD

Put the saffron in a small bowl, warm the milk to tepid and pour over the saffron strands.

Gently wash the rice in a large bowl with cold water (not under running water as this will break the tips of the rice, which will make the rice sticky). Change the water several times until it looks clear, then soak the rice in cold water for at least 30 minutes or up to 3 hours. Drain the rice well in a strainer.

Bring 1.5 litres water to the boil in a large pan. Add the rice once the water is boiling and boil until it is half done. It is hard to give an exact time for this as there are too many variables, but the way to check is to remove a single grain of rice from the hot water and squeeze it between your fingers – there should still be a hard core of slightly uncooked rice. Drain the half-cooked rice in a strainer and spread the rice thinly on a platter to cool and prevent it from continuing to cook.

Preheat the oven to 180°C/160°C fan/gas 4.

Heat the ghee or butter in a heavy-based pan over a medium–high heat. Add the cloves and cardamoms, followed by the pistachios, almonds and apricots. Add 250ml cold water and the sugar and stir until the sugar dissolves.

Butter a casserole dish and add the rice, then pour over the warm, spice-infused sugar syrup. Add the saffron-infused milk and stir gently to ensure the saffron is evenly distributed. Cover tightly with foil and bake for 15 minutes.

Take the dish out of the oven. Gently fluff the rice, then re-cover and bake for another 10–15 minutes. Remove the foil and leave the dessert to stand for a few minutes.

Sprinkle the kewra or rose water over the warm rice before serving.

# Lavender Sandesh

In Bengal, the use of *chenna* (milk curds) to make desserts goes back to the 16th century, after the Portuguese introduced cheese-making to the region. The origin of *sandesh* was a pragmatic way to use up excess milk that had gone off in the heat of Calcutta. By sweetening the milk curds, the Bengalis found a beautiful new dessert. It will keep, covered, in the fridge for a day or two.

I wanted to use lavender to flavour my *sandesh*. As I watched Tabitha (the prop stylist) arrange this beautiful shot, I suddenly remembered a shop in New Market in Calcutta. Their 'foreign' items were locked in a glass cabinet. I could not afford it but I was fascinated by the packaging and aroma of the Yardley Lavender Soap. I would ask them to take it out and show it to me; I would hold it and smell it and then return it. To me, in the middle of sultry New Market, that Yardley soap was what I imagined England would smell like. This picture reminded me of that, and my two worlds collided – a traditional Calcutta sweet dish looking like it belonged in that locked cabinet next to the Yardley soap!

## INGREDIENTS

about 500g *chenna* (see below)

150g caster sugar

1 tbsp fresh lavender flowers, crushed

### Chenna (makes 500g)

4 litres full-fat milk

120ml fresh lemon juice, strained

250ml hot water

## METHOD

First, make the *chenna*. Heat the milk in a heavy-based pan over a medium–high heat and bring it to the boil. Take the pan off the heat and wait until the bubbles subside, then pour in the lemon juice and stir in a clockwise direction. The milk should split and the curds will separate. If it does not split, add a little more lemon juice and stir in the same direction. If the curds still do not separate, warm the milk briefly until they do. Leave to settle for 5–10 minutes, then pour the hot water into the pan at the side, so it does not fall directly on the curds. Leave for 10 minutes.

Using a slotted spoon or skimmer, lift the curds into a muslin-lined colander. Tie the corners of the muslin and put a heavy weight on top to drain the curds. Leave for 20 minutes, then spread the curds on kitchen paper and gently pat with more kitchen paper to remove any remaining liquid.

To make the *sandesh,* mix the *chenna* curds with the sugar and lavender. Handful by handful, bray the curds, using the heel of your hand to break them down against the work surface (see the photograph overleaf, which demonstrates how this is done), until all the grainy texture is gone and the *chenna* is smooth.

Transfer the *chenna* to a heavy-based pan over a very low heat. Stir constantly with a wooden spoon until the *chenna* starts to look glossy and thickens – this should take 10–15 minutes.

Take the pan off the heat and leave until the mixture is cool enough to touch. Shape in decorative moulds or by hand before serving.

Above: My very glamorous maternal grandmother is inside the car here. This was probably Eid, as the three girls are wearing *gararas* (similar to what Amna and I wore for Arif's first birthday). Left to right: My aunt Rehana (Muni Khala as I call her), Afsana (Bhutan Khala) and Ammu.

# Rabri

## Milk Dessert with Pistachio

*Rabri* is a favourite winter wedding dessert, which is usually accompanied by *jalebi* or *gulab jamun*. Both those desserts are warm and syrupy, while *rabri* is thick, cold and creamy. If you really want to push the boat out, make the *rabri* when you make *Malpua* (page 116) and spoon a generous amount of *rabri* on top of the pancakes.

The key to perfect *rabri* is to source really good milk. Use full-fat (blue top) milk; any milk which is creamier than that would be even better.

SERVES 4

INGREDIENTS

1 litre full-fat milk

60g caster sugar

½ tsp seeds from green cardamom pods, crushed

1 tbsp rose water

3 tbsp unblanched shelled unsalted pistachios, finely chopped

METHOD

Heat the milk in a heavy-based pan over a high heat until it comes to the boil, then reduce the heat slightly to keep the milk at a steady rolling boil for 5 minutes. Turn the heat to low and leave the milk to simmer very gently, uncovered, for about 30–45 minutes, until the milk has reduced to one third of its original volume. When a skin forms, use a spoon to stick it to the side of the pan; you will need to do this repeatedly. Occasionally you will have to stir the bottom of the pan to ensure that the milk does not catch.

Towards the end of the cooking time, add the sugar and the crushed cardamom seeds. When the milk has reduced, take it off the heat and use a spoon to push all the skins from the side of the pan back into the milk. Leave to cool slightly before adding the rose water.

Spoon into a serving dish and place in the fridge to chill, preferably overnight Sprinkle the pistachios on top before serving.

# Celebration

food for big moments
and lots of people

**No celebration is complete without food.** In this chapter you will find dishes that were made to celebrate different occasions in my family, that you can cook to share and celebrate with loved ones, too. These recipes look stunning on the plate. My family reserve these for only the most precious occasions we are all together – weddings, birthdays and other similarly auspicious celebrations.

I was the first girl among my generation of cousins on the maternal side to go to college. I loved that my mother would not voice her concerns about my marriage to me. I know she must have been concerned when I turned 20 and there were no suitable boys in sight. Girls in my mother's family usually married when they were 18 or 19 years old. My mother had Amna when she was 19 and Amna also had her first child at 19. I will never forget my absolute amazement when I turned 19 and my mother offered to send me to Delhi to watch Bruce Springsteen in concert. Girls in my family were never allowed this kind of freedom. In the end, I did not go, but the fact that she offered to send me was a bigger deal than watching any concert. Ammu rarely said she loved me or said anything similar to my siblings. I would often catch her watching me and she would smile, tap the space next to her and invite me to sit with her. She would hold my hand in silence. I could feel the love but also her anxiety. We both knew a day would come very soon when I would get married and leave home. I would hear the chatter from people about me being too independently minded to make a good daughter-in-law. It clearly did not worry Ammu, as my parents were happy for me to work after I graduated. And then the inevitable happened… A suitable boy was found and my marriage was arranged.

There have been many special meals in my life, but there is one that I will never forget: it was my final meal at the house I grew up in, my parents' home. It was the night before I got married and, as is part of the ritual, my hands had been decorated with henna. The meal was one that I had requested specially (a treat because of my wedding the next day). Our cook Haji Saheb had make his famous *Sikandari Raan* (page 182). The food was ready and everybody else was eating – but my henna hadn't dried and I was getting impatient, and hungry. So my mother said, 'Okay, I'm going to feed you.' I sat there, under the tree in our garden, in my hand-dyed yellow sari, hands and feet covered with henna – and I was supposed to be so excited. But as she fed me, I wept. Traditionally, in our

Top left: At my *walima*, the wedding reception hosted by my in-laws in Dhaka, Bangladesh. I am wearing a *lehenga* which is a long skirt with a short top and a long *dupatta* or scarf.

Top right: My wedding in Calcutta. In my family, the tradition is to wear red on your wedding day. My *garara* (the wedding outfit) was made in my father's home in Aligarh, supervised by my mother.

Above: Ammu with two of her sisters, at a wedding in Calcutta.

Above right: My formal engagement in Dhaka, in my in-law's house. My mother-in-law gave me the gold bangle I am wearing in a small ceremony in front of her family and friends and introduced me to everyone. The smile is masking my nervousness. It was beginning to sink in that I was going to get married soon!

Right: Ammu and my lovely aunt Bhutun Khala (Afsana) getting me ready for my henna night in my parent's room in Calcutta. This was the night of my final meal in my parents' home.

Top: This was taken at my *haldi*, the purification ceremony before my wedding. This traditional ceremony is a blessing from all the women in the family who take turns to rub a turmeric paste on the hands and face of the bride-to-be.

Left: Amna and me in Hyderabadi *joras*, which are usually worn by the bride. They are also called *khada dupattas* and consist of a long tunic, *churidaar* (trousers) and a 6-yard-long *dupatta* (stole) that is draped around the body. We are also wearing traditional Hyderabadi jewellery.

Right: A *daawat* or feast at my parents' home in Aligarh. There is always a huge choice of food. Most of the women in my father's family do not eat meat, so Ammu cooks vegetarian dishes for them.

families, we are fed by hand when we are very young. Of course, I had no recollection of it. But that day, as I felt the touch of her fingers on my lips, I felt overwhelmed. I knew that this was her way of saying goodbye to me. And I realised that her way of showing love had always been to feed – but I had not understood until that moment. My mother was not the sort of person who spoke about her emotions. This is not unusual: ours was not a culture of hugging and kissing and telling children that you loved them. She herself was raised by a mother who didn't do that – so it simply didn't come naturally. But in that meal, I felt an entire lifetime of love.

A wedding celebration in my family would often have more than two thousand guests. *Chapli Kabab* (page 190) and *Kesar Pista Firni* (page 230) were often served at weddings, as it is easy to cook these dishes on a large scale. I remember the line of shallow terracotta plates being layered with *firni* to cool and set before the meal. Portioning the *firni* into individual bowls ensured that there were the right number of desserts for the guests invited, plus 50–100 additional portions for all the uninvited guests who would turn up! The practicalities of trying to chill a huge number of *firni* portions required children to be assigned to guard duty. The plates would be lined up on the floor and covered with fine muslin cloth to deter the flies, then the children were made to sit near the cooling desserts to stop the cats from getting their paws into them. The henna night and other meals before the actual wedding were much smaller gatherings, and the Rose, Apricot and Pistachio Pulao (page 212) and *Safed Murgh ka Saalan* (page 192) were popular dishes cooked for these meals, as they were milder and so could also be eaten by children. Cooking something with less chilli heat saved the cooks having to cook two different dishes, so any kind of korma is still something I associate with big family gatherings. It's a good tip for whenever you are cooking for large parties!

# Sikandari Raan

## Spiced Leg of Lamb

SERVES 6–8

This was the *raan* made the night before I left my home – my henna night – the meal my mother fed me by hand. In some ways, for me, that was the night of my biggest loss... leaving Ammu. But in my loss there lay ahead my victory – when I could recreate this meal for others; where I used food to empower myself and other women around me.

It is an auspicious dish that takes time to cook but it is worth the wait. The story behind this dish is that it was made for the defeated Indian king Porus by the chefs of Alexander the Great after the Battle of Hydaspes in 326 BC. The battle took place along the banks of the River Jhelum (which is now in modern-day Punjab in Pakistan). This special *raan* was made for a banquet to the honour the agreement between two kings. The original recipe is, of course, lost in the mists of time, so this is my family's version. The use of the local Himalayan pink salt and the pungent, sulphuric black salt, *kala namak*, is what makes this recipe so unusual.

This *raan* goes well with any bread, such as paratha or roti. For a special occasion, serve with Rose, Apricot and Pistachio Pulao (page 212).

### INGREDIENTS

2 small legs of spring lamb, about 1kg each (alternatively, use a shoulder of lamb or a medium leg of mutton or lamb, cut into 2 pieces)

200g ghee

*Marinade*

6 tbsp Himalayan pink salt

3 tbsp mild chilli powder

4 tbsp fresh lemon juice

4 tbsp ginger paste

4 tbsp garlic paste

2 tbsp black cumin seeds (*shah zeera*)

4 large Indian bay leaves (*tej patta*)

3 x 2.5-cm pieces of cassia bark

120ml malt vinegar

*Masala*

½ tsp cumin seeds

2 tsp fenugreek seeds

2.5-cm piece of cassia bark

2 cloves

2 green cardamom pods

1 tbsp white peppercorns

1 tsp *kala namak* (black salt)

2 tsp *amchur* (dried mango powder), or juice of ½ lime

*Method overleaf*

METHOD

Using a knife, make a couple of incisions on both sides of the lamb and release the meat from the bone at the top of each leg, so you can push some of the marinade between the bone and the meat. Rub the pink rock salt and chilli powder over the lamb. Put the legs into a sturdy roasting tin that you can use on the hob (you will need to reduce the liquid over the heat at a later stage). Mix the lemon juice with the ginger and garlic pastes and rub all over the lamb. Mix the black cumin, bay leaves and cassia bark with the vinegar, then rub this over the lamb too. Leave for 30 minutes, turning the legs in the vinegar and spice marinade and 'basting' the meat with the marinade at 10-minute intervals.

Preheat the oven to 180°C/160°C fan/gas 4. Cover the roasting tin with foil and cook undisturbed in the middle of the oven for 2½ hours.

To make the masala, dry roast the cumin and fenugreek seeds, cassia bark, cloves, cardamoms and peppercorns in a heavy-based pan over a low heat, stirring until they turn a few shades darker. Tip them onto a plate and leave to cool. Grind to a powder, using a spice grinder or a pestle and mortar.

Remove the tin from the oven and remove the foil. Melt the ghee and pour over the legs of lamb.

Put the roasting tin on the hob and bring the liquid to a slow rolling boil, turning the lamb once or twice, until the liquid is reduced. Turn off the heat.

To finish the masala, mix the black salt and *amchur* with the ground spices. Sprinkle the masala over the lamb and roll the legs in the roasting tin so all the remaining liquid sticks to the lamb. Taste, and if the seasoning needs to be adjusted, add more Himalayan pink salt.

To serve, place the lamb on a large serving plate and carve into thick slices at the table.

Above: In my bridal wear surrounded by flowers. The scent of lilies and gulab (rose) is one of my favourite floral fragrances. It always reminds me of the garland I wore at Hyderabad airport (see page 28) and of my wedding. Despite the associations with parting and leaving loved ones, I still love the fragrance.

# Shahi Paneer

## Paneer with Saffron and Cream

SERVES 6

In areas outside the lush green fields of Punjab – especially in the delta around the Bay of Bengal where there was not an abundance of grass – paneer was considered a luxury. This recipe was made for family gatherings on my father's side, where many of the women were vegetarian. My mother would always worry that the paneer would run out as everybody loved this – and it was meant to be a special dish just for the vegetarians. Of course, there was always more than enough. Paneer can be bland, so be brave with the salt on this one!

### INGREDIENTS

generous pinch of saffron strands

1 tsp rose water

6 tbsp vegetable oil

4 onions, thinly sliced

2 bay leaves

5-cm piece of cinnamon stick

4 green cardamom pods

4 cloves

1 tbsp garlic paste

1 tbsp ginger paste

2 tsp ground coriander

1 tsp chilli powder

120g full-fat Greek-style yoghurt

2 tsp salt

½ tsp sugar

100ml water

1 tbsp raisins

1kg paneer, cut into 5- x 2.5-cm pieces

1 tbsp slivered almonds

1 tbsp slivered pistachios

50ml thick or double cream

handful of toasted flaked almonds, to garnish

### METHOD

Soak the saffron strands in the rose water and set aside.

Heat the oil in a heavy-based pan over a medium–high heat. Add half the onions and cook, stirring, until they start to caramelise. Using a slotted spoon, remove the onions to a plate to cool, leaving as much of the oil in the pan as possible.

Add the bay leaves, cinnamon, cardamoms and cloves to the pan, along with the remaining onions, the garlic and ginger pastes, coriander, chilli powder, yoghurt, salt and sugar. Keep stirring, to prevent the onion mixture from burning and sticking to the base of the pan. Add the caramelised onions, water and raisins and bring to the boil, then lower the heat and keep the mixture at a slow rolling boil for a couple of minutes until the liquid has reduced and the oil has come to the surface.

Add the paneer and slivered nuts to the pan and cook for 2–3 minutes. Taste and adjust the seasoning, adding more salt if needed. Finally, stir in the saffron-infused rose water and the cream. Serve immediately, garnished with toasted flaked almonds.

# Shahi Gobi Saalan

SERVES 6

## Cauliflower in a Rich Coconut Gravy

This was a common celebratory dish, especially made for the large number of vegetarian matriarchs in my father's family. Family weddings and celebrations generally took place in winter so cauliflower always featured on the menu as a winter seasonal vegetable. Taking into account differences in cooking time, you can use this recipe to cook most vegetables. Sweet potatoes, yams, squash and carrots would all work. You could also use a combination of two vegetables. You can make this dish in advance and reheat over a low heat on the hob.

### INGREDIENTS

7 tbsp vegetable oil

1 large bay leaf

2.5-cm piece of cassia bark

2 green cardamom pods

1 clove

5 onions, thinly sliced

2 tbsp garlic paste

2 tbsp ginger paste

2 tsp ground coriander

1 tsp chilli powder

2 tsp salt

½ tsp sugar

250ml water

750g cauliflower florets, cut into 5-cm pieces

1–2 x 400-ml tins of full-fat coconut milk

6 tbsp ground almonds

handful of toasted flaked almonds, to garnish

### METHOD

Heat the oil in a heavy-based pan over a medium–high heat. Add the bay leaf, cassia bark, cardamoms and clove. The moment the clove starts to swell, add the onions, stirring to prevent them from sticking to the base of the pan. Cook until they start to caramelise.

Add the garlic and ginger and cook for 1 minute, then add the coriander and chilli powder and cook, stirring, for a further minute to ensure the spices are cooked through. If the mixture sticks to the base of the pan, add a splash of water. Add the salt and sugar, then pour in the water. Bring the mixture to the boil, then reduce to a slow rolling boil, stir, cover the pan and simmer until the oil comes to the sides of the pan.

Add the cauliflower and stir to coat all the pieces with the onion and spice mixture. Bring to the boil, then reduce the heat slightly, cover and cook for 4–5 minutes until the cauliflower is just cooked but still crisp. Taste and adjust the seasoning, adding more salt and sugar if needed.

Add 1½ tins of the coconut milk and the ground almonds and cook, uncovered, for 2–3 minutes. The thickness of tinned coconut milk varies so you may not need to add all of the second tin: you should have a creamy gravy, not too thin. Garnish with flaked almonds.

# Chapli Kabab

## Kabab from the North-West Frontier

SERVES 8

The name of this kabab comes from a Pashto word for 'flat'. Pashto is the language of the Pashtuns, who live in the region formerly known as the North-West Frontier, between Afghanistan and Pakistan. The popularity of the dish spread beyond the mountain regions into the cities of Pakistan and also became a favourite among certain families in Dhaka in Bangladesh. Part of Ammu's family migrated to Bangladesh from India in the 1960s and this kabab was frequently served at family weddings in Dhaka.

Our cook would sometimes add bone marrow for richness. It's optional, but I do recommend you try to get a marrow bone about 15cm long, split lengthways, and add the marrow to the mince mixture. This addition was authenticated by my friend Laila who I met in Cambridge: her family were from Swat in Waziristan, the rugged heartland where this kabab originated.

### INGREDIENTS

1½ tbsp pomegranate seeds

1½ tbsp coriander seeds

1½ tsp cumin seeds

150g onions, roughly chopped

150g tomatoes, roughly chopped

5-cm piece of fresh ginger, roughly chopped

4 green chillies, roughly chopped

50g fresh coriander, chopped

250g minced beef

500g minced lamb

bone marrow (optional, see introduction)

1½ tsp salt

100g cornflour

3 eggs, beaten

vegetable oil, for frying

### To Serve

red onions, sliced into rings

Khamiri Roti (page 162) or naan

### METHOD

Grind the pomegranate, coriander and cumin seeds together in a spice grinder.

Add the onions, tomatoes, ginger, green chillies and fresh coriander to a food processor and finely chop.

Put the minced meat and bone marrow in a large bowl. Add the dry spice mix, the onion and tomato mix, the salt, cornflour and beaten eggs and mix well. Oil your hands and divide the mixture into eight equal balls. Flatten to make kababs that are 9–10cm in diameter and 2.5cm thick.

Heat a 1cm depth of oil in a frying pan over a medium–low heat. Add the kababs in a single layer (you'll need to fry them in two or three batches) and fry for about 5 minutes on each side. Do not disturb the kababs as they fry or they may break; moving them may also lower the temperature of the oil.

Serve hot, sprinkled with salt and sliced red onions, with roti or naan.

# Safed Murgh ka Saalan

SERVES 4–6

## Chicken in White Gravy

This is a delicate chicken dish. In India, a whole chicken is almost always cut into pieces before cooking, and the skin is never left on. I was never sure how eight uneven-sized chicken pieces were shared by a family. My mother would always take the wing and insist that it was her favourite piece. I never realised the significance of this until I had children of my own and I would always want them to have the choicest pieces. I have suggested using chicken thighs in this recipe, but feel free to use a jointed whole chicken. Serve with *Sada Pulao* (page 198) or any other kind of delicately flavoured rice dish.

### INGREDIENTS

6 tbsp vegetable oil

1 large bay leaf

5-cm piece of cinnamon stick

2 green cardamom pods

2 cloves

250g onions, thinly sliced into half moons

2 tbsp ginger paste

1 tbsp garlic paste

1kg skinless chicken thighs, on the bone

1½ tsp salt, plus a pinch

300ml warm water

50g cashew nuts, finely ground

50g almonds, finely ground

400ml thick coconut milk

3 boiled eggs, cut into quarters, to garnish

### METHOD

Heat the oil in a heavy-based pan over a medium–high heat. Add the bay leaf, cinnamon, cardamoms and cloves and fry for a few seconds, stirring to prevent the spices from burning.

Add the onions and a pinch of salt and stir-fry for a couple of minutes, then lower the heat to medium–low and cook for 10–12 minutes until the onions are soft and translucent. The salt draws out the moisture from the onions and helps the process of sweating them; this is a pale dish and you do not want the onions to brown.

Add the ginger and garlic pastes, raise the heat to medium and stir for a minute. Add the chicken, 1½ teaspoons of salt and the water and bring to the boil, then lower the heat, cover and simmer for 20 minutes.

Remove the lid and turn the pieces of chicken around, add the cashew nuts and almonds and simmer uncovered for a further 10 minutes.

When the gravy has reduced and the oil has come to the surface, add the coconut milk, stir and simmer over a low heat for 5 minutes.

Taste and adjust the seasoning before serving. Garnish with boiled eggs.

# Zaffrani Raan

## Saffron Leg of Lamb

SERVES 6–8

This is a classic cash-rich, time-poor dish. The meat is expensive, but the process of marinating and cooking is very easy, although you will need to allow at least 4 hours to marinate the lamb. This is a good one to serve friends and family to make them feel loved without having to spend a lot of time in the kitchen! It is also a great dish to make when the cook has other responsibilities or little assistance to prepare the meal. This saffron-tinged meat will make an attractive centrepiece on the table.

Serve with the Rose, Apricot and Pistachio Pulao (page 212), with Gobi Masala (Spiced Cauliflower, page 144) and Anaras Jhal Chutney (Pineapple and Chilli Chutney, page 228).

### INGREDIENTS

2.5kg leg of lamb

8 garlic cloves, crushed

1¼ tsp chilli powder

400ml full-fat Greek-style yoghurt

2 tsp salt

1 tsp freshly ground black pepper

1 tsp saffron strands

400ml tepid water

40g butter, melted

### METHOD

Make a couple of incisions on both sides of the lamb. Mix the garlic, chilli powder and yoghurt with the salt and pepper, rub the mix over the lamb and leave to marinate in the fridge for a few hours. Meanwhile, soak the saffron in the tepid water for 2 hours.

Remove the lamb from the marinade and make five or six further incisions. Add half the saffron water to the marinade and then rub into the lamb, reserving about 6 tablespoons of the marinade. Leave the lamb to marinate for at least another 2 hours or preferably overnight in the fridge.

About an hour before you want to cook it, take the lamb out of the fridge and let it come to room temperature. Preheat the oven to 200°C/180°C fan/gas 6. Put a very large piece of foil in a roasting tin and put the lamb on the foil. Pour the melted butter over the lamb, followed by the remaining saffron water. Bring the foil over the lamb to make a sealed parcel and cook for 1 hour.

Open the foil and baste the lamb with the juices, then re-cover with foil and cook for a further 20 minutes.

Remove the foil and pour the reserved marinade over the meat. Cook for 20 minutes more, then leave in a warm place to rest for 20 minutes before carving. Serve the delicious roasting juices as a gravy to spoon over the meat.

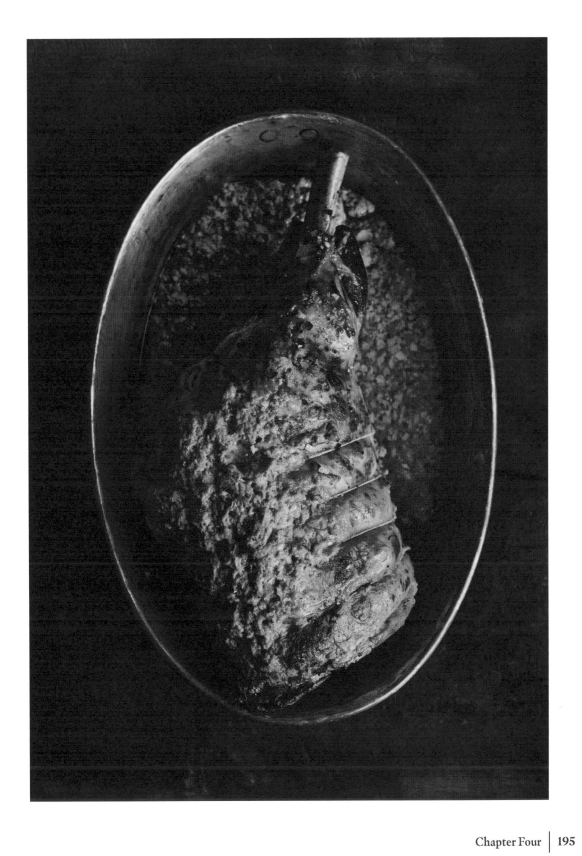

Above: This is one of my favourite pictures of Ammu, who is on the far left, with my uncle Parvez and her siblings. It looks like a vintage Bollywood film poster! Ammu loved bangles. The sound of her bangles tinkling together as she cooks has become the music of cooking for me.

Right: Ammu's bridal *tika* (headpiece) is at the top. It is inlaid with rubies and pearls, and was made in Karachi, Pakistan. Beneath it is my own headpiece, which is a vintage *tika* from Hyderabad, inlaid with uncut diamonds and Basra pearls.

# Sada Pulao

## Cashew Nut and Raisin Bengali Pulao

SERVES 4–5

The classic *sada pulao* of Bengal has a delicate fruity sweetness from the raisins. It is mostly cooked for weddings or festivals. You can replace the raisins with dried cranberries or apricots. If you discover a half-opened packet of dried fruits that are no longer as moist as they should be, make this pulao: the steam from the rice will bring them back to life. Serve with *Zaffrani Raan* (page 194), *Navratan Korma* (page 210) or *Hara Korma* (page 138).

### INGREDIENTS

300g basmati rice

5 tbsp vegetable oil or ghee

2 green cardamom pods

2.5-cm piece of cassia bark

2 cloves

1 large Indian bay leaf (*tej patta*)

50g cashew nuts

70g raisins or dried cranberries

1 small–medium white onion, thinly sliced

1 tsp salt

### METHOD

Wash the rice in a sieve under cold running water until the water runs clear, then place in a bowl of cold water to soak for at least 2 hours or for as long as possible – I always see a difference in the length of the grains after soaking. The grains will cook more quickly and are less likely to stick, as they absorb water while soaking.

Heat the oil or ghee in a heavy-based pan over a medium–high heat. When the oil is hot, add the cardamoms, cassia bark, cloves and bay leaf. After a few seconds, when the spices begin to sizzle and pop, use a slotted spoon to remove them to a plate, leaving as much of the oil in the pan as possible.

Add the cashew nuts to the pan and stir until they are lightly browned; remove with a slotted spoon and place on a plate.

Turn the heat to low, add the raisins/cranberries and cook for a few seconds – the moment they start to swell up, remove with a slotted spoon.

Add the onion to the pan and fry for 10 minutes, stirring occasionally, until golden brown and caramelised. Remove to a plate to drain. Spread the onion across the plate so it crisps as it cools.

Drain the rice and briefly spread on kitchen paper to remove any excess liquid – do not squeeze the grains, or they will break.

Put the kettle on to boil. Add the rice to the pan, then add the fried whole spices and half the caramelised onion. Stir for 1 minute to coat the rice in the spiced oil, add the salt and 600ml boiling water to cover the rice. Cook, uncovered, over a medium–high heat for about 4 minutes until the rice has absorbed most of the water. Reduce the heat, cover and simmer for a further 5 minutes until the rice is cooked.

Add the nuts and fruit and gently mix with a fork. Cover and leave for 5 minutes before serving. Garnish with the remaining onion.

# Machher Dopiyaza

## Fish with Double Onions

SERVES 6–8

Traditionally, we never ate fish in monsoon season. The wedding season, which was in the less humid and hot winter months, was the optimum time for fish-eating. This dish was made for most of our big family gatherings. It was also a dish much prized by the girls in our family, who had grown up eating fish in Calcutta but were married and now living in landlocked states where fish was not freely available. Ammu would always look out for my cousins in the crowd and make sure they got a good piece of fish to eat.

The challenge of serving fish at a large gathering was that people would have to be seated to eat. Most traditional fish dishes in Bengal were made with fish on the bone and trying to unpick bones while standing and holding a plate with one hand was not easy. In my home, this was made with fillets of *bhekti*, a local barramundi with white, flaky flesh. The thick onion gravy kept the fish moist.

Serve with plain boiled rice or *Sada Pulao* (page 198).

### INGREDIENTS

1 tsp ground turmeric

1½ tsp chilli powder

6 tbsp vegetable oil

2 large white onions, thinly sliced into half moons

2 tomatoes, chopped

1 tsp salt

1kg skinless halibut, plaice or tilapia fillets

green chillies, finely sliced, to garnish

### METHOD

Mix the turmeric and chilli powder with 2 tablespoons of water and set aside.

Heat the oil in a heavy-based frying pan over a medium heat. Add half the onions and fry gently, stirring occasionally, until softened but not browned.

Add the tomatoes, salt, the spice mix and the remaining onions and 50ml water. Raise the heat to high and cook for a few minutes until the raw smell of the spices has gone. If the mixture sticks to the base of the pan, add a splash more water.

Add the fish to the pan, bring the mixture to the boil, then cover and simmer for 5 minutes. Carefully turn the fish pieces over, cover and cook for a further 3 minutes.

Serve hot, garnished with sliced green chillies.

# Karai Murgh

## Chicken and Onion Cooked in a Karai

SERVES 4–6

In a traditional *daawat* (feast) in my home in India, we had to plan the menu for two kinds of guests – the rice-eating and the bread-eating. Most of Ammu's family were from regions that were primarily rice growing: the gravies were often thinner as they were meant to be mixed with rice and then eaten by hand. My father's family came from regions where wheat was grown: the gravies were much thicker, so it was easy to scoop up the meat and gravy with a piece of roti. This dish works best with rotis (page 162). You can replace the chicken with lamb or beef, in which case you would need to extend the marinating and cooking times.

### INGREDIENTS

3 tbsp coriander seeds

1 tbsp cumin seeds

1 tsp black peppercorns

1kg boneless, skinless chicken thighs, cut into 2.5-cm cubes

1kg full-fat Greek-style yoghurt

750g onions, finely chopped

2 tsp ground turmeric

6 tbsp ghee or oil

3 bay leaves

2.5-cm piece of cinnamon stick

10 dried red chillies, broken into two

4 green cardamom pods

4 cloves

8 garlic cloves, chopped

5-cm piece of fresh ginger, thinly sliced

1½ tsp salt

fresh coriander, to garnish

### METHOD

Dry roast the coriander, cumin and peppercorns in a heavy-based pan over a low heat, stirring until they turn a few shades darker. Tip onto a plate and leave to cool, then grind to a powder, using a spice grinder or a pestle and mortar.

Put the chicken in a large bowl, add the yoghurt, onions and turmeric and the roasted spice powder. Marinate for 30 minutes. (Red meat will need to marinate for 4 hours.) If the meat was marinated in a fridge, let it come to room temperature before you cook it.

Heat the ghee or oil in a *karai* or wok over a high heat. Reduce the heat to medium and add the bay leaves, cinnamon, dried red chillies, cardamoms and cloves. Stir for 30 seconds, then add the garlic and ginger and stir until they start to darken – but don't let them brown. Add the meat with its marinade, and the salt. Bring to the boil, then simmer uncovered over a low heat for 15 minutes. (If you are cooking red meat, cover and cook for 20–30 minutes until tender.)

Increase the heat and stir-fry until the liquid is reduced and the oil has come to the sides of the pan. Taste and add more salt if required. The gravy should be thick and clinging to the chicken. Serve hot, garnished with coriander.

# Golda Chingri Malaikari

## Prawns Cooked in Coconut Milk

SERVES 6

This is not an ordinary dish. Golda Chingri Malaikari was reserved for very special occasions. It was always served with plain boiled rice, and the dish arrived on the table with a grand flourish, the shells on the prawn heads glistening with the coconut gravy. As these prawns were very expensive and the prices fluctuated daily depending on the size of the catch and whether the day was auspicious for celebrations (which meant more buyers than prawns in the bazaar), my mother would buy these prawns herself and not leave the shopping to the cooks. We would go very early in the morning – just after dawn – to the local fish market, as the best prawns sold out quickly. They were usually 25–30cm from head to tail. My mother would ask the fishmonger to give me a stool to sit on before she started negotiating prices. I loved watching the cats in the market. They were sly and worked in gangs. There was an abundance of fish bones and bits of fish lying around on the floor, but their aim was much loftier: they would watch the live catfish in the shallow pools of water and try to pull one out to have a gourmet meal. While negotiating with my mother, the fishmonger kept swatting the cats swarming around the catfish pool; most of the time he would not even look down while swinging his hands around and I saw many close misses where the gang of cat thieves almost made off with a large fish!

### INGREDIENTS

1kg large raw prawns

2 tsp ground turmeric

2 tsp salt

2 onions

2.5-cm piece of cassia bark

2 green cardamom pods

2 cloves

4 tbsp ghee

2 tbsp vegetable oil

2 bay leaves

2 tbsp ginger paste

1 tbsp garlic paste

2 tsp mild chilli powder

100ml warm water

800ml thick coconut milk (tinned)

3 green chillies

½ tsp sugar

cooked rice, to serve

*Method overleaf*

## METHOD

Rinse the prawns and remove the shells from the bodies but keep the heads on. Mix half the turmeric and salt and rub all over the prawns; set aside.

Put the onions in a food processor and blitz to a paste; set aside.

Dry roast the cassia bark, cardamoms and cloves in a heavy-based pan over a low heat. As soon as the tips of the cloves start to swell and become a lighter shade of brown, immediately tip the spices onto a plate to cool. When the spices are cool, grind in a spice grinder. For this recipe you will only need 1 teaspoon. You can store any extra in a jar or in a small pouch of foil for about six weeks and use in recipes that call for garam masala.

Put a deep pan over a medium–high heat. Add the ghee and oil, then fry the prawns one at a time; when you pick up each prawn, give it a gentle shake to get rid of any liquid before you add it to the oil. Do not overcook the prawns: cook them quickly on both sides until they just turn opaque. Using a slotted spoon, transfer them to a plate as they are done.

To the ghee and oil remaining in the pan, add the onion paste and cook for 10 minutes. Add the bay leaves and the ginger and garlic pastes, the chilli powder, and the remaining turmeric and salt and cook for 3–5 minutes until the raw smell of the ginger and garlic has gone. Add the warm water and bring to the boil, then lower the heat and simmer until the oil comes to the surface, stirring to prevent the paste from sticking to the base of the pan.

Add the coconut milk and green chillies and bring back to the boil, then simmer, uncovered, for about 20 minutes, until thickened.

Add the prawns, lower the heat, cover and simmer for 5 minutes. Remove the lid, sprinkle in the sugar and 1 teaspoon of your garam masala and mix well. Serve with rice.

Top right: My maternal grandfather, Nana, was an avid photographer. He had converted one of the rooms in his section of the ancestral house into a dark room and occasionally he would allow the kids in to see the prints clipped on a wire to dry. He loved taking pictures outdoors. This was a family picnic in the Calcutta Botanical Garden. My family did not do things in half measures when it came to food, they would take huge pots of *pulao* or *biryani*, and tiffin carriers laden with food.

Bottom right: This photograph of Bapu entertaining guests hangs on the wall of the *sarkari burj* of my father's ancestral fortress. This room was part of the official tower where the head of the family had their living quarters. This picture was taken around 1912–14 at a time when Bapu was getting involved in politics. The size of the party indicates that this was a more informal gathering. Depending on the season, there would certainly have been *kofta* and *pulao* on the menu and the dessert would be *kheer*. Although, for the British guests, the cooks would make bread and butter pudding! I also heard stories that our family cooks would temper the *dal* with a gold *ashrafi* (coin) for a feast. My *dal* (page 90) is less glittery!

# Khaas Aloo

## Special Potatoes

SERVES 6

This dish was usually served at big family gatherings and everyone called it *khaas*, which means 'important' or 'special' in Urdu. We made it with small new potatoes, which was seen as a real treat, as the new waxy potato season was very short. Our everyday potato dishes were simple and anything added to the potatoes was usually something seasonal like fenugreek leaves or winter cauliflower. In this recipe, the nuts elevate a simple dish to a grand celebratory one. Delicious with *Zaffran Rogni Roti* (page 224) and *Lahsun Mirch Chutney* (page 156).

### INGREDIENTS

1kg waxy potatoes

6 tbsp vegetable oil

2 tbsp ghee

2 cloves

2 green cardamom pods

2 tbsp ground almonds

1 tbsp sesame seeds

4 green chillies

2.5-cm piece of fresh ginger, finely chopped

4 garlic cloves, finely chopped

1 tbsp cashew nuts

1 tsp ground turmeric

1 tbsp green raisins (in Indian grocery stores)

1 small onion, finely chopped

1½ tsp salt

250ml full-fat Greek-style yoghurt

flaked almonds, to garnish

### METHOD

Scrub the potatoes clean, leaving on any skin that remains intact. Cut the potatoes into 2.5-cm cubes. Prick with a fork. Heat the oil and ghee in a deep pan over a medium–high heat and fry the potatoes until they begin to turn golden brown, but do not cook them any further. Using a slotted spoon, remove the potatoes from the oil and leave to cool. Take the pan off the heat, keeping the oil in the pan.

Dry roast the cloves, cardamoms, ground almonds and sesame seeds in a heavy-based pan over a low heat. As soon as the spices start to darken, tip them onto a plate and leave to cool. Once cooled, grind the spices to a powder in a spice grinder.

Put the chillies, ginger and garlic in a blender with 4–6 tablespoons of water and blend to a paste. Mix the roasted spice powder with the paste and set aside.

Put the pan in which the potatoes were fried over a medium heat. Add the cashew nuts and turmeric, followed by the raisins, and stir very briefly – you do not want the raisins to swell and explode – then add the onion and fry until it starts to change colour. Add the spice paste, potatoes and salt. Stir to coat the potatoes in the spices, then add the yoghurt and 300ml water and bring to the boil. Lower the heat, cover and cook for 15 minutes.

Remove the lid and continue to cook until the sauce is clinging to the potatoes. Taste and add more salt if required. Garnish with flaked almonds.

# Navratan Korma

## Nine-Jewel Korma

SERVES 6

*Navratan* is a traditional South Asian style of gem-setting based on nine different precious stones. This korma is made up of nine colourful vegetables. It's a great way to use up odd veg from your fridge. Try red, yellow and orange peppers, aubergine, courgettes, baby sweetcorn, mangetout, cabbage and spinach. Or you could par-boil some carrots, parsnips, potatoes, French beans and pumpkin, then add red pepper, peas, sweetcorn and purple sprouting broccoli. A comforting, creamy (and extremely nutritious) curry that is ideal for children, too!

### INGREDIENTS

1kg mixed vegetables

6 tbsp vegetable oil

2.5-cm piece of cassia bark

2 green cardamom pods

1 clove

1 large bay leaf

2 large onions, cut in half and thinly sliced

3–4 garlic cloves, crushed

6-cm piece of fresh ginger, grated

2 tsp ground coriander

1 tsp chilli powder

½ tsp sugar

2 tsp salt

250g full-fat Greek-style yoghurt

400ml thick coconut milk

2 tbsp ground almonds

### METHOD

Cut all the vegetables into evenly sized pieces and set aside on a tray.

Heat the oil in a deep pan over a medium–high heat. Add the cassia bark, cardamoms, clove and bay leaf, then immediately add the onions and fry until golden brown.

Add the garlic and ginger and stir for 1 minute. Then add the ground coriander, chilli powder, sugar and salt and stir for 2 minutes.

Add the yoghurt, lower the heat to medium and stir until most of the liquid has evaporated. Add all the vegetables, stir and cook until tender. If the vegetables start to stick, add a splash of water. When they are cooked, add the coconut milk and ground almonds, and stir until the gravy thickens.

Taste and adjust the seasoning before serving. This korma goes very well with any kind of rice or pulao, and is a great accompaniment for meat or fish.

# Rose, Apricot and Pistachio Pulao

SERVES 6

This is not an everyday pulao, as the ingredients are expensive. If you can get good-quality pink food colouring, you can add some to a tablespoonful of the cooked rice in the final stages then mix it back into the pulao. This dish has sweet undertones, so it is best served with strong flavours and spicy/tangy dishes, such as *Sikandari Raan* (page 182), *Hariyali Murgh* (page 98) and *Karai Baingan* (page 100).

## INGREDIENTS

300g basmati rice

90g dried apricots, roughly chopped

70g shelled pistachios, roughly chopped

4 tbsp ghee or unsalted butter

2 green cardamom pods

2.5-cm piece of cinnamon stick

2 cloves

1 bay leaf

1 white onion, finely chopped

1 heaped tsp salt

good-quality pink food colouring (optional)

1 tsp rose water

rose petals, to garnish (optional)

## METHOD

Wash the rice in a sieve under cold running water until the water runs clear, then place in a bowl of cold water to soak for at least 2 hours.

Meanwhile, soak the apricots and pistachios in a separate bowl of cold water for 1 hour.

Heat the ghee or butter in a heavy-based pan over a medium–high heat. When hot, add the cardamoms, cinnamon, cloves and bay leaf. Stir-fry for a few seconds, then use a slotted spoon to remove all the spices to a plate, leaving as much ghee in the pan as possible.

Drain the apricots and pistachios and dry on kitchen paper. Add to the pan and cook for a couple of minutes. Remove with a slotted spoon.

Add the onion and fry over a medium–high heat, stirring until brown and caramelised. Remove the onion and spread over a plate.

Drain the rice and briefly spread on kitchen paper to remove any excess liquid – do not squeeze the grains, or they will break.

Put the kettle on to boil. Add the rice to the pan with the ghee, then add 600ml boiling water, the onion, the fried whole spices and the salt. Cook, uncovered, over a medium–high heat until the rice has absorbed most of the water.

If you want to include some pink rice, carefully remove 1 tablespoon of the rice and colour it, then return the pink grains to the main pan and stir through. Stir in the apricots and pistachios. Reduce the heat, cover and cook for a further 5 minutes. Remove the lid and sprinkle in the rose water.

Serve garnished with fresh rose petals, if using.

# Dum ki Murgh

## Baked Chicken

This chicken was usually cooked in a fire pit for large family gatherings at home. The smokiness from the charcoal pit added a great layer of aroma to the dish. As digging a hole in your backyard and cooking chicken over coal may not be an option for everyone, I have adapted the cooking process to use an oven and added the charcoal aroma by putting a smouldering coal into the oven in the final stages of the cooking. This *dhungar*, or smoking process, needs just one piece of hardwood coal a little bigger than a golf ball. The safest way is to burn the coal outdoors. If that isn't possible, you can hold the coal in tongs over a gas flame, turning it round so it is lit completely. Or use a blowtorch if you are comfortable using one. You could also cook this outside in a kettle or ceramic barbecue with a temperature gauge. It goes well with any kind of bread.

### INGREDIENTS

2 tbsp poppy seeds

25g cashew nuts

4 tbsp vegetable oil

2 onions, thinly sliced into half moons

300ml full-fat Greek-style yoghurt

4 tbsp thick or double cream

6-cm piece of fresh ginger, grated

1 tsp garam masala

1 tbsp ground coriander

2 tsp chilli powder

1 tsp salt

6 skinless chicken thighs, on the bone

### SERVES 6–8

*Dhungar*

1 piece of coal

skin of 1 large onion

small metal bowl

1 tbsp ghee or melted butter

### METHOD

Dry roast the poppy seeds and cashew nuts in a heavy-based pan over a low heat, stirring for about 2 minutes until the nuts start to darken, then tip them onto a plate and leave to cool. When cool, add a splash of water and grind to a paste, using a spice grinder or a pestle and mortar.

Heat the oil in a pan over a medium–high heat and fry the onions until they are caramelised. Using a slotted spoon, remove the onions from the pan, keeping as much of the oil as you can, and spread them on a plate to cool. Once the onions are cool, put them in a food processor and blitz to a paste.

Put the yoghurt and cream in a large dish. Add the onion paste, the poppy seed and cashew paste, the ginger, garam masala, coriander, chilli powder and salt. Add the oil in which the onions were fried (ensure it has cooled before you add it).

Add the chicken to the yoghurt mix and marinate for at least 4 hours. If you marinate it overnight in the fridge, ensure you bring the chicken to room temperature before cooking.

*Continues overleaf*

Preheat the oven to 180°C/160°C fan/gas 4. Line a roasting tin with a large piece of foil – large enough to enclose the chicken and make a little tent over the roasting tin. Lay the chicken in a single layer in the tin and cover as much of the chicken with the marinade as possible. Close the foil over the chicken to seal, then bake for 45 minutes.

While the chicken is baking, prepare the coal for the *dhungar* so it is ready to go in the oven. You can burn it outdoors or over a gas flame. Let the coal burn for 5–6 minutes and wait until it starts to go grey around the edges. Layer the onion skin in a small metal bowl and put the burning ember inside.

This last part is a bit tricky. Open the oven door, remove the roasting tin and put it down on a safe surface. Carefully open the foil covering (do not tear as you will need to cover again). Create a space in the middle of the chicken pieces to fit the metal bowl. Put the metal bowl with the smouldering ember inside the roasting tin. Pour the ghee into the bowl (this will create the smoke) and immediately close the foil cover as quickly as you can to maximise the smoke impact. Put the chicken back in the oven for another 10 minutes.

Open the foil covering and cook for a further 15 minutes.

Serve immediately.

# Karela Bhaja

## Fried Bitter Gourd

SERVES 4

A dish made with a bitter vegetable may not seem to be a delicacy or celebratory dish for most people, but for many Bengalis, karela or bitter gourd (*pictured on page 72*) is a much-loved vegetable and considered to be the ideal way to start a feast. Karela, served with some plain boiled rice, is used as a palate cleanser and is a good way to prepare for a rich and complex meal. There are, of course, many health benefits linked to karela, too, the most popular being the reduction of blood sugar levels in diabetics. In my home, my father would eat karela purely for the medicinal benefits, but Ammu enjoyed the indulgence of a proper Bengali meal with fish (such as *Machher Dopiaza*, page 200) and *bhortas* (see page 218) and rice with karela. My husband and my son Ariz also love this dish. The salting step is very important as it helps to reduce the bitterness of the vegetable. In Bengal, it would traditionally be prepared with mustard oil, but as it is not available everywhere, I use vegetable oil instead.

### INGREDIENTS

250g bitter gourd (also known as *karela* or bitter melon, it can be found in Asian grocers, or frozen in supermarkets)

¼ tsp salt

½ tsp ground turmeric

½ tsp chilli powder

4 tbsp vegetable oil (or mustard oil)

2 whole dried red chillies

boiled rice, to serve

### METHOD

Thinly slice the bitter gourd into rounds, about 1cm wide, and remove the seeds. Place in a bowl and mix with the salt, then cover with a plate and set aside for 20 minutes.

Squeeze the bitter gourd slices to remove any excess liquid and transfer to a plate lined with kitchen paper. This is an important step, as the salt removes the bitter juices from the vegetable. Discard the liquid. Pat the slices dry, then sprinkle with the turmeric and chilli powder and mix until they are evenly coated.

Heat the oil in a shallow saucepan or frying pan over a high heat for 2–3 minutes, then reduce the heat to medium and heat for a further minute. (If you are using mustard oil, heat it over a high heat until it reaches smoking point, then reduce the heat. The high temperature reduces the pungent flavour of mustard oil.) Add the whole dried red chillies and stir for a few seconds until the chillies have darkened, then add the bitter gourd slices. Cook, stirring, until they turn dark brown and crisp around the edges. Remove from the pan with a slotted spoon.

Serve with boiled rice.

# Tomato Bhorta

## Spicy Mashed Tomatoes

*Bhorta* or *bharta* is a generic term used in Bengal to describe anything that has been minced, pounded, or chopped up into very small pieces. It is a side dish almost like a relish, which is commonly eaten with rice and lentils. This *bhorta* goes really well with *Bhuna Khichuri* (page 134).

No Bengali New Year celebration in Bangladesh is complete without various kinds of *bhorta*. If tomatoes are available, this *bhorta* will definitely be on the table.

As it has a salsa type of texture, it can be used as a relish for burgers or even grilled halloumi. It's a great accompaniment to barbecued meats, too. It can be made in advance and kept covered in the fridge for 24 hours until you are ready to eat.

SERVES 6–8

INGREDIENTS

8 ripe tomatoes

4 green chillies, finely chopped

2 white onions, finely chopped

1 tbsp oil (preferably mustard oil)

¾ tsp salt

chopped fresh coriander, to garnish

METHOD

There is a messy way to roast the tomatoes, using direct heat – either by cooking them on the embers of a barbecue or by holding them in tongs directly in a flame, turning them so they roast evenly. These methods give an added smokiness, but they are not always practical. The easiest way is to heat up a *tawa* or a griddle over a high heat and roast the tomatoes on it until the skins are blackened.

Once they are cool enough to handle, remove the skins and chop the tomatoes into small pieces.

Mix the tomatoes with the chillies, onions, oil and salt and serve chilled or at room temperature, garnished with coriander.

# Hasher Mangsho Bhuna

## Spicy Duck Curry

SERVES 4

My family in Bangladesh usually serve this with *Chhita Roti* (page 222). When I was young, I do not remember seeing duck served at any of my family dinners in India. Both duck and duck eggs were traditionally popular in certain regions of Bangladesh. Recently, its popularity has grown and you can get a lot more duck in Dhaka, the capital city, and in the rest of the country. The reason for the increased use of ducks is an environmental one: the country has large pockets of *haors* – wetlands, which are linked to the rise in sea levels and frequent flooding of parts of the country. Ducks can swim, chickens cannot.

### INGREDIENTS

4 duck legs (around 1kg)

120ml malt vinegar

1 tsp salt

120ml vegetable oil

2 onions, thinly sliced into half moons

250ml water

1 tbsp garlic paste

1 tbsp ginger paste

1 tsp chilli powder

1 tsp ground turmeric

1 tsp ground coriander

1 tsp ground cumin

### METHOD

Put the duck in a bowl with the vinegar and salt and leave to marinate overnight. Bring the duck to room temperature before cooking.

Heat the oil in a heavy-based pan over a medium–high heat. Add the onions and stir-fry for a couple of minutes. Add the water followed by the garlic, ginger, chilli powder, turmeric, coriander and cumin and stir until the raw smell of the garlic and ginger has gone.

Remove the duck from its marinade, add to the pan and cook over a high heat until the legs are browned. Add water to just cover the duck and bring to the boil, then lower the heat, cover the pan and simmer for 45 minutes–1 hour until the duck is tender.

Remove the lid and cook over a high heat to remove any excess liquid until the sauce reaches your preferred consistency.

# Chhita Roti

## Lacy Rice Flour Roti

SERVES 4–6

This is a wonderful gluten-free roti from Bangladesh. Part of my mother's family moved to present-day Bangladesh in the 1960s and our family owned a tea garden in Sylhet. This roti was prepared in the tea garden for special occasions and it always accompanied a spicy and tangy duck curry (page 220). Making the roti is a messy process, so keep a damp cloth to hand to wipe away splashes of rice flour that may go all over the cooker. If you want to include green chillies and fresh coriander, you should chop them very finely so they do not detract from the lacy look of the roti. It can be used as an accompanying bread with any of the recipes in this book.

A lot of people who eat in Indian restaurants think Indians eat naans at home. No, we do not. In almost every region of India, it is almost unheard of for a family to use a tandoor to cook bread on a daily basis, for the very practical reason that not everyone has an outdoor space to have a smoky wood- and coal-burning oven. Also, to burn all that fuel to cook bread for a small family would be impractical. Most of the daily bread made at home is cooked on a *tawa*, like this roti. This is a lesser-known bread from South Asia and definitely worth adding to your usual repertoire.

### INGREDIENTS

250g rice flour

½ tsp salt

350ml water

1–2 green chillies, finely chopped (optional)

2–3 tbsp finely chopped fresh coriander (optional)

4 tbsp vegetable oil

### METHOD

Put the rice flour and salt in a bowl and gradually whisk in the water to make a smooth, thin batter – like the batter you would make for a crêpe. If using, stir in the chopped green chillies and coriander.

Set a *tawa* or frying pan over a medium heat. Use a pastry brush or a clean piece of cloth to dip into the oil and spread a thin film on the heated surface. Using your fingers or a spoon, make sprays of the batter on the *tawa*. Move your fingers or spoon in such a way as to create a lacy pattern, but fill in large gaps, as you need the roti to hold together. When cooked, the roti will become opaque. Lift with a spatula or palette knife and fold into quarters.

This roti is best eaten hot from the *tawa*.

# Zaffran Rogni Roti

## Saffron-infused Bread

SERVES 6 (MAKES 12 ROTIS)

Adding saffron to this roti gives it a beautiful colour and also a delicate flavour and aroma. Saffron is the most celebrated but also, in my opinion, the most abused spice today. I have been served food that should never have saffron in it, like a cumin-infused pulao with saffron – two flavours that contradict rather than complement each other. Often the need to impress guests (especially at a wedding!) sees saffron being added to almost everything, just because it is such a precious and expensive spice. With the rising popularity of the spice and predatory pricing, along with other challenges, it is now hard to find Kashmiri saffron. It is impossible to judge the flavour and colour of saffron until you infuse it. Never go by the hard sell of the shopkeeper or the packaging – the only way to find great saffron is to try it yourself; once you find a good one, go back and buy more and keep it in your cupboard!

This bread goes well with any kabab from this book and also with *Bhuna Niramish* (page 254) and *Khatteh Ande* (page 42).

INGREDIENTS

450g plain flour, plus extra for dusting

1 tsp salt

240ml warm milk, plus 1 tbsp for soaking the saffron

generous pinch of saffron strands

6 tsp ghee or melted butter

METHOD

Mix the flour and salt in a bowl and gradually add the warm milk to make a soft but not sticky dough. Cover and set aside for at least 30 minutes, or up to 2 hours.

Meanwhile, soak the saffron in 1 tablespoon of warm milk in a small bowl for at least 30 minutes.

Add the saffron-infused milk to the dough and knead the dough on a lightly floured surface for 4–5 minutes. Divide into 12 equal pieces, shape each piece into a ball, then place on a plate, cover with a clean damp kitchen cloth and set aside for 30 minutes.

Put a *tawa* or frying pan over a medium heat. On a lightly oiled surface, roll out each dough ball to a 15-cm circle. Take a knife and make 1-cm slashes into the circle to prevent the bread from puffing up while cooking. Add a drizzle of ghee or butter to the pan and cook each roti for 30–45 seconds on each side until brown spots appear. Brush both sides of the roti with melted ghee or butter after cooking.

# Chingri Bhorta

## Spicy Mashed Prawns

A *bhorta* is not meant to be a substantial side dish. It is a tangy and often spicy little relish, which is served alongside a simple meal of rice and dal. Even if one of the ingredients is cooked, the others will almost always be fresh raw ingredients.

In this recipe, small prawns are cooked quickly and then mixed with onions and spices to make an inexpensive and tasty addition to a meal. In my family, we always have this *bhorta* with plain rice.

SERVES 4–6

INGREDIENTS

½ tsp ground turmeric

½ tsp chilli powder

1 tsp salt

500g raw peeled small prawns

2 onions, finely chopped

2 green chillies, finely chopped

2 tbsp mustard oil

1 tbsp chopped fresh coriander

1 tbsp vegetable oil

METHOD

Rub the turmeric, chilli powder and salt on the prawns and leave to marinate for 20 minutes.

Combine the onions, chillies, mustard oil and coriander in a bowl.

Heat a *karai* or wok over a medium–high heat, add the oil and then stir-fry the prawns until they are just cooked. Remove from the heat and pound the prawns with the back of a spoon to break them up.

Transfer the prawns to the bowl with the onions and chillies and mix well. Taste and adjust the seasoning before serving.

# Anaras Jhal Chutney

## Pineapple and Chilli Chutney

Pineapple chunks with rock salt and tangy *chaat masala* sprinkled on top was a popular roadside snack in Calcutta. I was never allowed to eat it, as the sweet aroma of the pineapples and the sticky juice that dripped from the stand always attracted a lot of flies, who would sit on the fruits. Even with all the enthusiasm of youth and that feeling of invincibility, I could see it was probably not the safest thing to eat. This spicy pineapple chutney is my homage to that street food I never got to eat.

### INGREDIENTS

1 sweet pineapple

1 tbsp vegetable oil

3 dried red chillies, broken in half

2 Indian bay leaves (*tej patta*)

2.5-cm piece of fresh ginger, grated or cut into thin slivers

2 tbsp sugar

1 tsp rock salt

350ml water

### METHOD

Cut the skin off the pineapple and cut out all the hard 'eyes', then cut the pineapple into small cubes. Have a plate or container ready to collect the juice that comes out of the pineapple – this can be added to the chutney.

Heat the oil in a deep pan over a medium–high heat. Add the chillies, followed by the bay leaves and ginger and stir for a few seconds until the ginger starts to darken – you do not want it to brown. Add the pineapple chunks, sugar and salt and stir for a few minutes, then add the water. Let the mixture come to the boil, then reduce the heat and simmer, uncovered, until the chutney thickens and looks glossy.

Taste and add more salt or sugar if required. Serve warm or at room temperature.

This can be kept in a sealed container in the fridge for 2–3 days.

# Kesar Pista Firni

SERVES 6–8

## Saffron and Pistachio Rice Dessert

This rice and milk dessert is made in my family for larger gatherings such as weddings or Eid. If you are not expecting guests all day and plan to serve the *firni* at the end of the meal, you can make it in one bowl, although I love serving it in individual dishes. It can be eaten warm but is best served cold.

### INGREDIENTS

100g basmati rice

100g shelled unsalted pistachios

2 litres full-fat milk

100ml double cream

¼ tsp saffron strands

1 Indian bay leaf (*tej patta*)

1 green cardamom pod

320g white granulated sugar

### To Decorate

handful of pistachios, cut into slivers

rose petals (optional)

### METHOD

Wash the rice in cold water and leave to soak in the water for 2–4 hours.

Drain the rice, then pour it onto a tray and pat dry with kitchen paper. Spread the rice on layers of kitchen paper and leave for 30 minutes to get as much of the moisture out as possible. When it looks dry, grind to a powder in a grinder or blender.

Put the pistachios in a bowl, add boiling water to cover and leave to soak for 10 minutes. Drain and gently rub the nuts with a clean cloth to remove the skins. Place back in the bowl, add cold water to cover and leave to soak for another 20 minutes. Drain and whizz in a blender with 500ml of the milk.

In a small pan, gently warm the cream until tepid, then remove from the heat, add the saffron and set aside to infuse.

Add the pistachio milk to the remaining milk in a heavy-based or non-stick pan. Bring to the boil, then reduce to a slow rolling boil. Add the bay leaf and cardamom pod, stirring to prevent the milk from sticking to the base of the pan. After 15 minutes add the powdered rice, bring the milk back to the boil, then reduce to a slow rolling boil again. The rice may stick around the edges of the pan, so scrape it up and push it back into the milk. Any skin that forms while the milk is boiling should be broken and pushed back into the milk. The mixture should take about 30 minutes to thicken.

Add the sugar to the hot milk and stir until it has dissolved. Add the saffron-infused cream and gently mix, then immediately pour into a serving dish or individual dishes. As it cools it will form a top layer, which in many families is considered the best part of the dessert. Once cooled, place in the fridge to chill, preferably overnight. Decorate with pistachio slivers or rose petals.

# Sheer Korma

## Vermicelli Eid Dessert

SERVES 4–6

This is a traditional dessert of milk, nuts and vermicelli, which is served on the morning of Eid in many households in the Indian subcontinent. It is best served warm, but you can also serve it chilled.

The dates give this dessert a beautiful caramel-like flavour. For many, this sweet, warming, milky dessert – which in our house was usually served in delicate bone china cups – was the first breakfast after 30 days of fasting over Ramadan. I have often wondered if the boiling of dried dates was a way to use up dates that the family had left over from the stock they would have kept for the ritual breaking of the fast with a date during Ramadan. You will need to boil the dates the night before you make this. If you cannot find *chuwara*, look for dried dates that are not plump or glistening. Ideally, you want a date that looks dehydrated. Seviyan is a wheat vermicelli that is usually roasted, ready to use in desserts: look for it in Asian stores.

### INGREDIENTS

4 dried dates (*chuwara*)

1.6 litres full-fat milk

100g roasted seviyan or fine wheat vermicelli

4 whole blanched almonds

4 shelled unsalted pistachios (or ½ tsp slivered pistachios)

5g fresh coconut (optional)

40g ghee or unsalted butter

2 cloves

2 green cardamom pods

200g caster sugar

1 tbsp cashew nuts, split in half

1 tbsp raisins

### METHOD

The day before making the dessert, put the dried dates in a pan with 240ml of the milk, bring to the boil and then simmer for 20 minutes. Leave to cool, then chill.

If you haven't got roasted seviyan you will need to dry roast the vermicelli over a low heat until it starts to darken.

Cut the almonds (and pistachios, if using whole ones) into slivers. If including coconut, chop the flesh into 1.5cm cubes. Break the vermicelli into small pieces.

Put the remaining milk in a pan, add the soaked dates and their milk and bring to the boil.

Meanwhile, heat half the ghee or butter in a frying pan over a medium–high heat and flash-fry the vermicelli with the cloves and cardamoms, then add to the boiling milk. Add the sugar and stir until it has dissolved. Take the pan off the heat and discard the cloves and cardamoms.

In a separate frying pan, heat the remaining ghee and quickly fry the almonds, pistachios, coconut, cashews and raisins until the nuts darken – you do not want to burn them. Add the mixture to the vermicelli, reserving a little to sprinkle on top if you like. Serve the milky vermicelli warm or chilled in individual glass dishes.

# Being Ammu

quick, modern recipes
for instant solace

**When I became a mother, I took on my own role as Ammu.** These are the recipes I make for and also with my children, teaching them how to cook. A fusion of western ingredients and Indian spices, these recipes make good, practical and quick meals for all ages.

When my older son was 4 years old, he suddenly developed a very British accent. He had been going to nursery school for a few months, but I had clearly missed the transformation. I immediately called my parents and made Ariz speak to them. My mother was very bemused, but my song-for-every-occasion father started singing a vintage Bollywood song: '*Mera Jootha hai Japani, Yeh Patloon Englistani, Sar pe Laal Topi Rusi, Phir bhi dil Hain Hindustani.*' The translation of this 1955 hit goes: 'My shoes are Japanese, these pants are British, I have a Russian hat on my head, but my heart remains Indian.' My father told me my child may now dress and speak differently from me, but he will remain a Hindustani (Indian).

My parents were in London when both my boys were born, and Ariz and Fariz have developed a close bond with their grandparents over the years. They are also close to my husband's mother who lives in Dhaka. The principal source of communication between the grandparents and my children is food – their language of love. The summers we went home, Ammu would personally select the mangoes for my youngest son. He would hold her hand and go to the storeroom where the large baskets of the orchard mangoes were stored. My mother would sort them by checking the aroma of each mango and judging when it would ripen. Just like my father taught me how to select a good mango, Ammu taught Fariz so he could pick one for himself when she was not with him. The image of my little boy huddled over the mango baskets, listening intently to Ammu, is an image I will carry in my heart forever.

My mother would visit often when my boys were young and pick them up from school. She would cook for them and introduced them to classic Calcutta colonial-inspired dishes and Calcutta Haka food. I have shared two of the Calcutta Haka food recipes in this chapter (pages 260–262). Fusion food became a feature: the Pakoras (page 244), *Jhal* Steak (page 252) and Chicken Kabab Burger (page 246) all combine elements of western food traditions with Indian spicing. As time went on, the practicalities of the two children eating at different times from me and my husband made it necessary for me to cook things that they could eat cold, such as *Lobia* (page 266), or could reheat easily, such as *Keema Puffs* (page 258).

Top right: Ariz and me in Holland Park – one of our favourite places for an outing when he was young. Ariz loved going to the rose garden and watching the koi fish in the Japanese garden. Emotional and kind, even as a small child, he could pick up on tension and try to comfort me.

Middle left: Fariz was born 5 years after Ariz. Fariz is neat and organised. He was born that way! When he was very young, I gave him a chocolate-covered raisin from a jar that had other things in it. I watched as he systematically emptied the jar, set aside all the chocolate raisins for himself, then put everything back in the jar and returned it to me!

Middle right: I spent a lot of time alone with Ariz in his early months as my husband was away a lot looking after his father who was very unwell. Whenever it rained, I would make him sit near the window and we would watch the rain together. I would sing the songs my father would sing to me when it rained in Calcutta during the monsoons.

Bottom left: My boys have a beautiful bond. They rarely argue and have remained very close as they have grown up. This is one of my favourite pictures, Fariz anchoring himself on his older brother.

Having grown up in a nuclear family and away from my clan of relatives, both kids found large family gatherings intimidating and were never keen to attend family weddings. They don't understand why I love being in a room with loud aunties all talking at the same time! As children, they would only occasionally wear traditional Indian clothes and were clearly uncomfortable in them. Last Eid was the first time they both came out to eat dinner dressed in traditional Kurta pyjamas. Ironically, our dinner that day was the *Sikandari Raan* from this very book! I had been at the photoshoot all day and took the leg of lamb home for them. Somehow, that meal felt like a turning point. Now aged 21 and 16, Ariz and Fariz seemed very emotional eating a dish that had been made by my family for me on my last night at home before I got married.

Something changed that night. Even though it was just four of us around the table, it felt as if it was not just Eid but a much larger celebration. Every night after the photoshoot, I would share the pictures of the food we had taken and would tell my sons the stories behind the dishes. While writing this book and telling my children about the food my mother cooked, I felt my children were understanding me more. The effort they took to dress up and eat at the table as a family was unusual. I do not know when my boys will meet with the rest of my family and break bread with my clan but that night I felt as though they understood their culinary heritage better. They understood how food was about love and happiness, and made an effort to dress up in the traditional way my family would dress in India, to make that meal feel more special.

There is an anecdote I remember from my childhood: On one of my walks with my father through our family mango orchard, I asked him why he had planted the saplings so far apart. He told me that you must have *umeed*, which means 'hope' in Arabic, that the saplings will grow up to be big, strong trees. You need to nourish them, pray that they get sunshine and rain and you need to give them space to grow and flourish. You had to hope and believe that the young trees were growing strong roots below to weather the storms. My father's philosophy that you have to give a tree the space to grow and lengthen its roots is something I have adapted to my children and what they eat. I know their roots will eventually make them understand and value Indian food. At the moment, I am giving them the space to discover themselves and find their way home.

Top left: Ammu cooking *keema* (recipe on page 256) with Ariz in my London home. Ariz cooks *keema* a lot when he is at university.

Top right: Eid in Calcutta, around 2002. My mother had decided to give the staff the day off and we had gone to Saturday Club for a fish and chips lunch. I love that Ammu never did things because it was expected. She always prioritised family time over ceremony and tradition.

Bottom left: Ariz was too young to understand the significance of the cap my father had put on him. This was in Calcutta and we were leaving to head back to London that day. Abbu took out Bapu's prayer cap from his bedside table where he kept the letters his grandfather had written to him. I knew how much this prayer cap meant to Abbu. Bapu was a *hafiz* of the *Quran* (he could recite it from memory) – a deeply spiritual man. Of all the personal things of his grandfather that were offered to him after he had passed away, all Abbu had taken was this prayer cap and Bapu's dressing gown.

Bottom right: Ariz was so spoiled by Ammu when he visited India. She would cook especially for him and then feed him. She still cooks for both my boys when they visit. I know this is her way of communicating love.

# Paneer Kofta

## Indian Cheese Balls

A fantastic kofta dish for vegetarians, this came out of several unsuccessful early attempts at making paneer with the help of my eldest son Ariz. The end result was a rather sad crumbly cheese that did not become compact. I made this kofta with it, as I remembered that Ammu would often use the crumbly edges of the paneer she made to make this dish. I eventually learned how to make the perfect paneer and now have to crumble it up to make this.

### INGREDIENTS

1 slice of bread, crusts removed

500g paneer, crumbled

1 tsp salt

3 tbsp chopped fresh coriander

5 green chillies, chopped (fewer if you don't like it too hot), plus 2 whole green chillies, to garnish

1 clove, ground

¼ tsp each freshly roasted and ground cardamom and cassia bark
(or ½ tsp ground cinnamon)

1 small white onion, finely chopped

1 egg, beaten

vegetable oil, for deep-frying

*Sauce*

5 tbsp vegetable oil

2 dried red chillies, broken in half

2 cloves

1 green cardamom pod

3 onions, chopped

SERVES 6

1½ tsp ginger paste

1½ tsp garlic paste

¼ tsp ground turmeric

2 tsp ground coriander

2 tbsp tomato purée

### METHOD

Soak the bread in cold water, then squeeze out all the liquid, break it up and place in a bowl. Mix with the paneer and the remaining kofta ingredients. Shape the mixture into small ovals, each about the size of a golf ball.

Fill a deep, heavy-based pan or wok no more than one-third full of oil. Heat until it is hot but not smoking; test by adding a cube of bread – it should brown in 30 seconds. Deep-fry the kofta in batches until they darken, then set them aside to drain on kitchen paper.

To make the sauce, heat the oil in a pan over a medium–high heat, add the dried red chillies, cloves, cardamom, onions and the ginger and garlic pastes, and fry until the onions are golden brown. Add the turmeric and coriander and cook for 30 seconds, then add 2 tablespoons of water to prevent the onions and spices from burning. Reduce the heat, then add the tomato purée and cook until the oil separates from the mixture. Add 250ml water and simmer for 2–3 minutes.

Just before you are ready to serve, add the kofta to the sauce and turn them around very gently a few times. They break easily, so don't move them too much. Garnish with green chillies and serve with pulao or bread.

# Lamb Seekh Kabab

SERVES 6–8 (MAKES ABOUT 30 KABABS)

Lamb seekh kabab was a speciality dish made in my father's family. My aunt Tabby Chachi was the expert. This recipe is close to what my aunt makes but not quite the same. None of us will ask her what that magic ingredient is that she puts in her dish! This is my family recipe, which I hope my boys will learn one day and make in their own kitchens. It is very versatile and goes well with a simple salad like the *Lobia* (page 266) or with a potato dish, such as *Baghare Aloo* (page 104) or the more elaborate *Khaas Aloo* (page 208). It is quick to cook and great to prepare when you are entertaining, as all the prep can be done in advance and the kabab can be cooked at the last minute.

## INGREDIENTS

2 tbsp gram flour (besan)

1kg lean minced lamb

2 tbsp ginger paste

2 onions (about 250g), finely chopped

1 tbsp Kashmiri or medium chilli powder

2 green chillies, finely chopped

1 egg, beaten

2 tbsp full-fat Greek-style yoghurt

4 tbsp chopped coriander leaves

1 tsp garam masala

2 tsp salt

4 tbsp ghee, melted butter or vegetable oil

*Garnish (optional)*

onions, sliced into rings, lime or lemon wedges, whole green chillies

## METHOD

In a cast-iron frying pan or heavy-based pan, dry roast the gram flour over a medium–high heat, stirring continuously to prevent it from burning, until it loses its raw smell and darkens a couple of shades. Put the roasted flour in a bowl, add all the remaining ingredients (except the ghee/butter/oil) and mix well to form a paste-like consistency.

You can cook the kababs on a barbecue or an indoor grill. If using a barbecue, wait until the coal has reduced to glowing embers. If cooking indoors, preheat the grill to medium–low. Line the grill tray with foil.

You will need about 30 metal skewers (*seekh*) to cook the kababs. Oil your hands, as the mixture will be sticky, and divide the mix into about 30 balls. Insert a skewer into the middle of each ball, then press tightly along the skewer until you have a 5–6cm 'tube' of meat. Leave 6cm of space at the top of the skewer: if you leave too much space it will be more difficult to take the kabab off the skewer.

Cook on the barbecue or grill, turning frequently to ensure even cooking and basting with the ghee, butter or oil. (If easier, you can gently ease out the skewers and arrange the kababs on a foil-lined baking tin.) Once the kababs start to darken, after 7–8 minutes, increase the grill heat to high and cook for a further 7 minutes.

Serve with a garnish of sliced onions, lime or lemon wedges and whole green chillies.

# Buttermilk Chicken Pakoras

SERVES 4–6

This is a halfway house between a chicken nugget and a spicy pakora, which is sold in *dhabas*, or roadside eateries, along the Indian highway. These are very delicious and can also be fried in a deep-fat fryer, if you have one. My boys use random dips with these pakoras, including mayonnaise. If you are serving this as a starter, it may be nice to serve it with the Coriander and Mint Chutney (page 35) or the Raw Mango Chutney (page 158).

## INGREDIENTS

1kg boneless skinless chicken thighs, cut into 2.5-cm cubes

500ml buttermilk

2 cloves

2.5-cm piece of cinnamon stick

2 bay leaves

3 tsp fennel seeds

3 green cardamom pods

2 tsp salt

150g rice flour

1 tsp ground cumin

1½ tsp chilli powder

125ml full-fat Greek-style yoghurt

vegetable oil, for deep-frying

## METHOD

Put the chicken in a pan with the buttermilk, cloves, cinnamon, bay leaves, fennel seeds, cardamoms and 1 teaspoon of the salt. Bring to the boil, then reduce the heat and simmer, uncovered, for about 20 minutes until the chicken is cooked and tender. To check, take out one piece of chicken and cut it in half to ensure it is no longer pink in the middle. Remove the chicken from the buttermilk and spread out on a plate. Strain the liquid and keep aside; discard the spices.

Put the rice flour in a bowl, add the cumin, chilli powder and the remaining salt and whisk in 200ml of the strained buttermilk, followed by the yoghurt, until evenly combined.

Heat the oil in a deep pan over a high heat. Drop a little of the batter into the oil to test if it is ready – it should immediately start to sizzle and darken. If the oil is not hot enough, heat it for a bit longer and test again. Using a slotted spoon, remove the trial batter and lower the heat to medium. Do not fry pakoras over a high heat as the outside will burn and the inside of the batter will remain raw.

Dip the chicken pieces in the batter, ensuring they are totally covered, and then fry the pakoras in the hot oil in small batches. Do not overfill the pan as that will reduce the temperature of the oil and the pakoras will not get crisp. Drain on kitchen paper as you take each batch out of the oil. Serve hot.

# Chicken Kabab Burgers

Similar to the iconic bun kabab of Karachi in Pakistan or Hyderabad in India, a spicy kabab inside a bun is a popular street food in certain regions of the Indian subcontinent. You can add Pineapple and Chilli Chutney (page 228), Coriander and Mint Chutney (page 35) or Garlic and Chilli Chutney (page 156). These kababs can also be cooked on the barbecue. You could use minced beef or lamb instead of chicken, but you may need to adjust the cooking time.

## INGREDIENTS

750g minced chicken thighs

1 tbsp full-fat Greek-style yoghurt

1 tbsp ginger paste

1 tsp garlic paste

1 tsp chilli powder

1 tsp ground coriander

1 tsp garam masala

½ tsp freshly ground black pepper

1 tsp salt

3 green chillies, finely chopped

1 onion, finely chopped

2 small tomatoes, chopped

2 tbsp chopped coriander leaves

1 egg, beaten

200ml vegetable oil, for frying

*To Serve*

12 burger buns (or naan or pitta bread)

chutney (optional)

1 red onion, sliced into 12 rings

## METHOD

Put the minced chicken in a bowl and add all the remaining ingredients (except the oil); mix well. Oil your hands and divide the mixture into 12 pieces. Roll each piece into a ball and then flatten to a patty. Each kabab should be 2cm high. Cover the kababs to prevent them from drying out.

Heat the oil in a frying pan over a high heat. To test that the oil is hot, cut one of the onion slices in half and dip the tip into the oil – it should start to sizzle immediately. If not, heat the oil for a bit longer and check again. Reduce the heat to medium and after 30 seconds slip the kababs in from the edge to prevent the oil from splashing and burning your hand. Do not overload the pan. Fry the kababs in a single layer with enough space for you to turn them safely, until well browned on both sides and cooked through.

Slice open the burger buns and spread both sides with a thin layer of chutney, if using. Top with a kabab and a slice of onion.

# Honey and Soy Chicken Skewers

SERVES 4

The combination of honey and soy sauce is so Calcutta! Bengali food is known for the 'touch of sugar' that is added to savoury dishes to balance the flavours. The use of soy sauce was common in many households because of the Chinese influence, and soy sauce made locally in Chinatown in Calcutta was hugely popular. I have had a version of this kabab where the cook added a generous pinch of chilli flakes to the marinade: if you like your kabab spicy you can try that! The kabab can be cooked on an indoor grill or on a barbecue. It's delicious served with paratha or other bread.

## INGREDIENTS

4-cm piece of fresh ginger

2 garlic cloves

6 tbsp light soy sauce

1½ tbsp white wine vinegar or fresh lime juice

1 tbsp clear honey

1 tsp ground coriander

1 tsp Kashmiri chilli powder or mild chilli powder

500g boneless skinless chicken thighs, cut into 2.5-cm cubes

## METHOD

Crush the ginger and garlic in a pestle and mortar or a food processor, then add the soy sauce, vinegar or lime juice, honey and spices to make a marinade.

Put the chicken in a bowl, add the marinade and mix well to ensure all the pieces are coated. Cover the bowl and leave to marinate in the fridge for at least 2 hours or preferably overnight.

If you are using an indoor grill, it is better to use bamboo skewers: soak them in water for 20–30 minutes before threading the chicken. When cooking on a barbecue, I prefer to use metal skewers. Bring the chicken to room temperature before cooking. Divide the pieces among four skewers. Thread the chicken pieces onto the skewers so that all the meat will be under the heat.

Ideally, the skewers should be 10–15cm away from the heat source. The chicken must cook all the way through, so it shouldn't be too close to the heat source or the outside will burn, leaving the inside raw. Grill the skewers for about 5 minutes on each side. Once the chicken is browned, cut a piece in half to ensure it is cooked all the way through.

# Eggs with Spiced Tomato Gravy

SERVES 4

This is a perfect dish if you need to cook a satisfying meal in under 30 minutes and do not have a lot of ingredients to hand. If you have a glut of tomatoes from your allotment or garden, this is a good way to use up some of the tomatoes that may be getting a bit overripe. If you do not have fresh tomatoes, you can substitute tinned tomatoes; drained whole plum tomatoes are better than chopped ones, which have too much liquid and take longer to cook down. You could add a tin of sweetcorn to the gravy, and instead of the eggs you could add mozzarella and finish it under the grill.

## INGREDIENTS

6 tbsp vegetable oil

3 whole dried red chillies

6 garlic cloves, cut into thick slivers

1.25kg fresh tomatoes, roughly chopped

½ tsp sugar

1½ tsp salt

4 eggs

chopped fresh coriander, to garnish

## METHOD

Heat the oil in a deep frying pan over a medium–high heat. Add the dried chillies, followed by the garlic, and stir-fry for a few minutes. Add the tomatoes, sugar and salt and cook, uncovered, for about 10 minutes, until you can see the oil coming to the sides of the pan.

Carefully break the eggs into the tomato gravy. Cover, reduce the heat and cook until the eggs are done to your liking. Garnish with coriander.

# Jhal Steak

*Jhal* means spicy in Bengali and this steak has been inspired by the chilli beef sold in small roadside eateries in India's only Chinatown, Tangra in Calcutta. This dish is my homage to my childhood and the incredible culinary influences on the cuisine of my hometown. In Calcutta in the 1980s, there was an abundance of places where you could get excellent beef steak, from the iconic Skyroom on Park Street to the refined dining rooms of Calcutta Club and Saturday Club. Both my boys love steak and mash. This is my Calcutta tweak.

## INGREDIENTS

2 steaks, about 200–250g each

2 tbsp soy sauce

1 tbsp white wine vinegar

½ tsp ground ginger

1 or 2 garlic cloves, crushed

1 tbsp chopped green chillies (green finger chillies are ideal; if you are using bird's eye chillies, use ½–1 tsp)

¼ tsp brown sugar

vegetable oil, for frying

### Spiced Garlic and Chilli Mash

400g white potatoes

4 tbsp salted butter

1 bay leaf

1 dried red chilli, broken into small pieces

2 garlic cloves, thinly sliced

¼ tsp salt

## METHOD

Put the steaks in a shallow dish. Combine the soy sauce, vinegar, ginger, garlic, chillies and sugar and pour over the steaks; turning the steaks to coat them in the marinade. Cover and set aside in the fridge for at least 2 hours, or overnight. Bring the steaks to room temperature before frying.

To make the mash, boil the potatoes in their skins, with a pinch of salt. While the potatoes are still warm but cool enough to handle, remove the skins. Mash the potatoes until smooth, using a masher or fork. Warm the butter in a small pan over a medium heat, add the bay leaf, the dried red chilli and the garlic, stirring until the garlic starts to brown – but don't let it burn. Pour the contents of the pan over the mashed potatoes and mix. Remove the bay leaf. Add the salt, then taste and adjust the seasoning to your liking. Keep warm while you cook the steaks.

Preheat a non-stick pan or griddle over a high heat. Add a drizzle of oil then add the steaks and cook for 2 minutes on each side, adding a touch more oil when you flip the steak. Cook one steak at a time if you find that easier; wipe the pan with kitchen paper after cooking the first steak to remove any residue. When they're done, put the steaks on a plate and cover with foil to rest for a few minutes before serving with the mash.

# Bhuna Niramish

## Shredded Cabbage with Peanuts

SERVES 6–8

*Niramish* is a classic Bengal vegetable dish that can be made with any kind of vegetable. The name means something 'without meat or flesh'. This was a popular dish for home cooks as it could be made just before mealtimes and did not require much preparation. *Niramish* was made with vegetables at the height of their season, when there was a glut and the prices were low. This recipe works best with a vegetable that can be shredded and cooked quickly by stir-frying in a *karai* or wok. You can add shredded fennel or grated carrots to the cabbage if you want. The peanuts give an added crunch to the dish and the additional protein from the peanuts makes my older son happy – he is an amateur boxer and trains every day.

### INGREDIENTS

4 tbsp vegetable oil

125g raw peanuts

½ tsp mustard seeds

1 bay leaf

1 tbsp grated fresh ginger

2 green chillies, slit in half

about 800g cabbage, shredded

1 tsp salt

1 tsp ground turmeric

1 tsp ground cumin

1 tsp ground coriander

generous pinch of sugar

### METHOD

Heat the oil in a *karai* or wok over a medium–high heat. Have a plate and slotted spoon ready next to the cooker. Add the peanuts to the oil and stir-fry for a few seconds until they turn a couple of shades darker. Take care not to burn the peanuts: you cannot take your eyes off them. Using a slotted spoon, remove the peanuts to a plate, leaving as much of the oil in the pan as possible. Spread the peanuts across the plate to cool.

Add the mustard seeds to the oil in the pan and wait until you hear the 'popping' sound before adding the bay leaf and ginger. Stir-fry until you can smell the ginger aroma – the colour of the ginger should not change. Add the green chillies and cabbage and stir-fry for a couple of minutes, then add the salt, turmeric, cumin, coriander and sugar. Lower the heat so that the cabbage does not stick to the pan and stir-fry until the cabbage is cooked.

Sprinkle the peanuts over the cabbage.

# Keema Mattar

## Minced Beef with Peas

We would eat *keema* at least twice a week when I was a child. My brother was a fussy eater: he would not eat whole pieces of meat and barely ate chicken unless it was boneless. He loved *keema* though, and the cooks would make it often as it was convenient to stuff into toasties for us when we came home from school. Many years after leaving India I realised that *keema* was very much a family dish; it was probably not considered sophisticated enough to serve to guests. In large families, *keema* was an economical way to feed everyone some meat. Buying ready-minced meat means that this is a convenient dish to make for the family.

### INGREDIENTS

½ tsp cumin seeds

2 tbsp vegetable oil

2 green cardamom pods

2.5-cm piece of cassia bark

2 dried red chillies

2 small Indian bay leaves (*tej patta*)

1 onion, finely chopped

1 tsp ginger paste

½ tsp garlic paste

500g minced beef (10 per cent fat)

½ tsp ground turmeric

1 tsp ground coriander

¼ tsp chilli powder

¾ tsp salt

1 tbsp tomato purée

75ml hot water

50g frozen peas

1 tbsp fresh lemon juice

fresh mint leaves, to garnish

### METHOD

Dry roast the cumin seeds in a heavy-based pan over a low heat, stirring until they turn a few shades darker. Tip them onto a plate and leave to cool. Grind to a powder, using a spice grinder or a pestle and mortar.

Heat 2 tablespoons oil in a pan over a medium–high heat. Add the cardamoms, cassia, dried chillies and bay leaves, immediately followed by the chopped onion. Stir the onion for a minute and then add the ginger and garlic pastes and stir for a further minute.

Add the minced beef and break it up with the back of the spoon to ensure it does not cook in clumps. Add the ground cumin seeds, turmeric, coriander, chilli powder and salt and cook the mince, uncovered, until all the liquid from the meat has evaporated. Add the tomato purée and the hot water and bring the mixture to the boil, then lower the heat, cover the pan and simmer for 5 minutes.

Remove the lid, add the frozen peas and cook until the mince looks quite dry. Taste and adjust the seasoning, adding more salt if required.

Add the lemon juice and stir through; garnish with mint.

# Keema Puffs

## Minced Beef and Potato Patties

Both my boys love pies. For them, the keema puff I make is a 'mama style of pie'. A legacy of colonial times, patties and puffs with meat or vegetable filling were very popular in Calcutta. The chicken patties of Flurys on Park Street were legendary and something I always looked forward to eating when I returned to see my parents in the 1990s. You can use this recipe for any leftovers you have in the house. Instead of potatoes you could add a tin of drained cooked beans to the meat. Or you can make a vegetarian filling. What is important is that the filling should have no liquid – it should be moist but not wet, otherwise the patties will be soggy.

### INGREDIENTS

150g leftover cooked Keema Mattar (page 256)
100g boiled potatoes, cut into small cubes
salt and freshly ground black pepper
500g ready-rolled puff pastry

1 egg, beaten

### METHOD

Line a baking sheet with baking parchment.

Warm the keema and add the chopped cooked potatoes. Season to taste with salt and pepper. Leave the mixture cool.

Cut the puff pastry into six squares. Put about 2 tablespoons of the filling in the middle of a square. Avoid overfilling or filling too close to the edge, or the patties may open up during cooking. Using a pastry brush or your finger, wet all round the pastry square with water. Fold the pastry over the filling to form a triangle. Press down along the edge to seal the triangle. Continue to fill and seal all the remaining patties.

Transfer the patties to the baking sheet. Use a damp fork to seal the edges again. Place in the fridge and chill for 30 minutes.

Preheat the oven to 190°C/170°C fan/gas 5. Brush the patties with the beaten egg. Bake for 40 minutes until the patties are golden brown and the filling hot. Depending on the size and personality of your oven, you may need to turn the baking sheet around halfway through cooking to ensure the patties cook evenly.

Serve warm. Tomato ketchup is a good accompaniment to this dish.

# Mushroom Hakka Chow

## Calcutta-style Noodles

SERVES 4

The arrival of the first Chinese immigrant to Calcutta was recorded in 1778, when a Mr Yang Tai Chow set up a sugar factory near Calcutta (the Bengali word for sugar is 'chinni', which also means Chinese). Apart from sugar, the most significant contribution by the Chinese to Bengal was their food. Calcutta is the city where I was born and spent most of my childhood. The Calcutta Haka food of Calcutta is unique: the confusingly named 'red sauce' is actually locally produced, dark brown, slightly sweet soy sauce and it gives Hakka Chow in Calcutta a wonderful flavour. Whenever we went out to eat in India we would almost always go to a Chinese restaurant, and Hakka Chow was what I always ordered. In college I looked forward to the days when Chinese noodles were on the menu. After moving to England in 1991, I was so disappointed with the Chinese food available here, and on one of my trips back to India I learned how to cook Hakka Chow by watching a vendor cook the noodles in his street cart. I add brown sugar to the noodles to replicate the red sauce used in Calcutta. Before I opened the restaurant, I would cook Hakka Chow at least twice a week for my family in London. Now it is our Sunday dinner.

### INGREDIENTS

250g flat or portobello mushrooms

1 large carrot, about 100g

1 red pepper

250g dried egg noodles (or more depending on hunger!)

3 tbsp vegetable oil

200g white onions, thinly sliced

6 garlic cloves, crushed

¼ tsp salt

½ tsp freshly ground white pepper

5 tbsp dark soy sauce

½ tsp brown sugar

thinly sliced spring onions, to garnish

### METHOD

Cut the mushrooms into thick strips. Cut the carrot and pepper into strips about 5–8cm long and similar in thickness to the mushrooms.

Cook the noodles according to the packet instructions, then rinse in cold water, drain and set aside.

Heat an empty wok until smoking hot. Add the oil and then immediately add the onions, red pepper and carrot strips, garlic, salt and pepper and stir-fry for a minute. Add the mushroom strips and cook for 2 minutes or until the mushrooms look glossy. Add the drained noodles, soy sauce and sugar and cook for a further 2–3 minutes. Taste and adjust the seasoning.

Serve immediately, garnished with spring onions.

# Calcutta Haka Chilli Chicken

SERVES 4

Whenever I visit India I always try to make a trip to Tangra, which is the Chinatown in Calcutta, to eat Chilli Chicken and Hakka Chow. My mother would make this as a way to get my younger son Fariz to eat with the family, as he was never too keen on Indian food. Calcutta Haka food is probably my children's favourite cuisine. I'm not sure whether it's because my mother made it for them when they were young or because I make it so often as it's so quick and easy. This is a one-dish meal, but it satisfies the whole family. Serve with Hakka Chow (page 260), too, if you like.

## INGREDIENTS

500g boneless skinless chicken thighs, cut into 2.5-cm chunks

5 tbsp soy sauce

2.5-cm piece of fresh ginger, grated

2 garlic cloves, finely chopped

1 large egg, lightly beaten

vegetable oil, for frying

2 dried red chillies

4 tbsp plain flour

2 onions, thinly sliced into half moons

2 tbsp cold water

1½ tsp cornflour

2 green peppers, sliced into strips

2 tbsp chopped green chillies

¼ tsp sugar

## METHOD

Mix the chicken in a bowl with the soy sauce, ginger and garlic. Set aside for 30 minutes.

After 30 minutes, add the egg to the bowl and stir to coat the chicken evenly.

Heat a 4cm depth of oil in a *karai* or wok over a medium–high heat. Add the dried chillies and stir until they darken and give out a smoky aroma. Remove with a slotted spoon, leaving as much oil in the pan as possible.

Dip the chicken in the flour to coat it, then fry in the hot oil until cooked. Do not crowd the pan and fry the chicken in batches so there is adequate space to stir the pieces around. To check that it's cooked, cut a piece of chicken in half to ensure it is no longer pink in the middle. Using a slotted spoon, remove the chicken and drain on kitchen paper.

Pour off all but 2 tablespoons of oil from the pan and place over a medium–high heat. Fry the onions until they are translucent. Meanwhile, in a small bowl, mix the water with the cornflour until smooth.

Add the green peppers to the onion pan and stir-fry for 1 minute (do not overcook them). Add the cornflour mix to the pan, then add the chopped green chillies and keep stirring until the sauce thickens.

Return the fried chicken pieces and red chillies to the pan and stir until the chicken is coated with the sauce. Stir in the sugar, taste and add more soy sauce if you like. Serve immediately.

# Chennar Mattar Bhurji

## Scrambled Cheese and Peas

SERVES 4

An alternative to scrambled eggs, this is a healthy and satisfying meal that can be put together very quickly. Commercially bought paneer or cottage cheese can be used, but home-made *chenna* makes it very special.

This dish is useful when you discover the box of eggs next to the cooker is empty – one of the boys somehow ate the remaining six eggs that were there the night before, but he left the empty box where it was to confuse you!

### INGREDIENTS

3 tbsp butter

2 green chillies, chopped

1 onion, chopped

¼ tsp ground turmeric

½ tsp dried fenugreek leaves (*kasur methi*)

1 tomato, chopped

300g *Chenna* (page 170; paneer or cottage cheese can be used instead)

100g frozen peas, defrosted (or drained tinned sweetcorn)

½ tsp salt

3 tbsp double cream

3 tbsp coriander leaves, to garnish

### METHOD

Heat the butter in a frying pan over a medium–high heat, add the chillies, followed by the onion, turmeric, fenugreek leaves and tomato and stir-fry for 3–4 minutes.

Add the *chenna* and peas and cook for 4 minutes. Turn off the heat, add the salt and cream and mix gently. Taste and adjust the seasoning before serving, garnished with the coriander leaves.

# Lobia

## Black-eyed Bean Salad

You need to soak black-eyed beans overnight in water before cooking. Although they are readily available in tins, I prefer to soak and cook dried beans, as they do not have the metallic smell that tinned beans often have. Lobia releases sugars slowly and is a very healthy addition to the boys' diet – trying to remind them to eat the salad leaves in the fridge can get tedious. This is a lovely textured salad and you can add other bits to it, including grilled halloumi, paneer, boiled eggs or pickled beetroot or shallots.

SERVES 4

INGREDIENTS

200g dried black-eyed beans

2 garlic cloves, chopped

½ small onion, chopped

1 green chilli, chopped

1 red tomato, diced

2 tbsp olive oil

2 tbsp fresh lime juice

1 tsp brown sugar

salt and freshly ground black pepper

METHOD

Soak the beans in cold water overnight.

The next day, drain the beans and put them in a pan, cover with fresh water and bring to the boil. Cover the pan and simmer for about an hour, until they are soft. Drain and leave to cool.

Put the beans in a bowl, add the garlic, onion, chilli and tomato and mix to combine. Whisk the olive oil, lime juice, sugar, salt and pepper together, pour into the bowl and mix to combine.

# Khosha Chorchori

## Fried Vegetable Skins

SERVES 3–4

A 'no-waste' traditional Bengali dish, where potato, gourd and pumpkin skins are fried with green chillies and onions. It's traditionally flavoured with *panch phoran*, a mix of five spices. When my son helps peel vegetables, he does take a lot of the veg off too. This dish (I often make it just with potato skins) makes everyone happy as nothing is thrown away. This chorchori is not meant to be a complete side dish but something extra to lift your meal. The recipe can be used to cook any vegetable – finely cut – so it's perfect for using up any stray vegetables you may find in your fridge.

### INGREDIENTS

250g peels of pumpkins, potatoes, courgettes

2 tbsp vegetable oil

¼ tsp panch phoran

2 onions, thinly sliced

2 green chillies, slit in half

2 dried red chillies, broken in half

1 tsp ground turmeric

½ tsp salt

### METHOD

Wash the vegetable peels well and cut into thin julienne strips.

Heat the oil in a frying pan over a medium–high heat. Add the panch phoran, followed by the onions and green chillies and stir-fry for a couple of minutes.

Add the dried red chillies and turmeric, then the vegetable peel and salt. Stir-fry until the strips of peel are tender.

# Saag Baadam

## Spinach with Roasted Almonds

Spinach with roasted almonds is a great combination. The addition of the nuts gives this spinach dish a nice crunch and also boosts its nutritional value. Both of my boys love garlic and I have added a generous amount, but you can reduce it to suit your taste. I am not a fan of kale, but if you like it you can substitute kale for the spinach.

SERVES 4–6

### INGREDIENTS

4 tbsp olive oil

2 dried red chillies

8 garlic cloves, crushed

1 red pepper, cut into small pieces

1kg fresh spinach leaves

½ tsp salt

100g roasted unsalted almonds, cut into slivers

### METHOD

In a deep pan that is large enough to hold the spinach, heat the olive oil over a medium–high heat. Add the dried chillies (leave them whole if you just want the smoky chilli flavour; break in half if you want the spinach to be more spicy) and cook for a few seconds, then add the garlic and red pepper and stir for 1 minute. Add the spinach and salt and cook until the spinach has wilted and any excess water has evaporated.

Sprinkle the almonds over the spinach before serving.

# Channa Pulao

## Chickpea Pulao

SERVES 6

This is a good storecupboard meal, which can be put together quickly. I am happy to eat carbs on carbs, but if you want to add some protein to your rice, this is a great recipe. Soaking tinned chickpeas in water removes the 'tinny' smell. For the quantity of chickpeas you need for this recipe, it is not worth the effort of soaking and cooking dried ones. In India, we call cream-coloured chickpeas *Kabuli chana*, 'chickpeas from Kabul'. They are a relative newcomer to our cuisine, introduced from Afghanistan two centuries ago. I sometimes wish I could go back in time to the ancient bazaars of Delhi or the ports of Calcutta or Chittagong and see how people responded to a new ingredient, why they cooked something the way they did. Did the trader selling the new ingredient suggest recipes? Today, it is so easy to learn how to cook with a new ingredient thanks to the internet. Centuries ago, it must have been so mysterious and exciting to cook with something new.

### INGREDIENTS

600g basmati rice

400-g tin of chickpeas, drained

6 tbsp ghee or unsalted butter

3 green cardamom pods

5-cm piece of cinnamon stick

3 cloves

1 bay leaf

2 white onions, finely chopped

2 tsp salt

### METHOD

Wash the rice in a sieve under cold running water until the water runs clear, then place in a bowl of cold water to soak for at least 2 hours. Meanwhile, soak the chickpeas in a separate bowl of cold water for 30 minutes.

Drain the chickpeas and dry on kitchen paper.

Heat the ghee or butter in a pan over a medium–high heat. Add the cardamoms, cinnamon, cloves and bay leaf and fry, stirring, for a few seconds. Using a slotted spoon, remove all the spices to a plate, leaving as much ghee in the pan as possible. Add the drained chickpeas to the pan and cook for a couple of minutes. Remove with a slotted spoon and place on the plate with the spices.

Add the onions to the pan and fry, stirring, until brown and caramelised. Remove with a slotted spoon and place on the plate.

Put the kettle on to boil. Drain the rice and briefly spread on kitchen paper to remove any excess liquid – do not squeeze the grains, or they will break. Add the rice to the ghee in the pan, followed by 1.2 litres of boiling water from the kettle, the caramelised onions, the fried whole spices, chickpeas and salt. Cook, uncovered, over a medium–high heat until the rice has absorbed most of the water.

Reduce the heat, cover the pan and cook for a further 5 minutes. Turn off the heat and leave the rice undisturbed for 5 minutes.

Gently loosen the rice, turning it with a fork, and serve warm.

# Adrak Phulli

## French Beans with Ginger

These beans can be eaten warm or cold. I usually cook double the quantity so there are leftovers for the next day. I have noticed the boys will open the fridge and stare inside and then close the door without taking anything out. Not wanting to label them as lazy, but I noticed that, most days, they do not pick anything to eat from the fridge that requires reheating or assembling! Having a vegetable leftover in the fridge that can be eaten hot or cold is convenient.

SERVES 4

INGREDIENTS

250g French beans

1 tsp vegetable oil

1 tsp sesame seeds

2.5-cm piece of fresh ginger, finely grated

½ tsp salt

100ml warm water

1 tbsp fresh lemon juice

2 tsp chopped mint leaves

METHOD

Wash, top and tail the beans and cut them into 1-cm pieces. Heat the oil in a wok or deep pan over a medium–high heat, add the sesame seeds and stir-fry for a few seconds. Add the ginger, beans and salt and stir-fry for 3–4 minutes.

Add the water and bring to the boil, then cover and cook for 8–10 minutes.

Remove the lid and cook until any remaining liquid has evaporated. Add the lemon juice, then taste and adjust the seasoning. Garnish with the mint leaves.

# Dum ki Macchi

## Steamed Fish

As the traditional banana leaf to wrap and steam the fish is not always on hand, I sometimes steam the fish in foil. Banana leaves are available in most Asian shops selling fruit and vegetables, so do use them if you can find them.

Many of the traditional fish curries I grew up eating had bones. The legendary *ilish maach* of Bengal, with its slender bones, was a real challenge to navigate: it was easier when eating with your hands as you could feel for the bones instead of looking for them! Until my sons perfect the art of eating a fish packed with bones, I cook this fish dish for them.

Serve with *Channa Pulao* (page 272) as a great way to make a quick and efficient family meal.

**SERVES 6**

### INGREDIENTS

6 small pieces of haddock fillet

6 tbsp white vinegar

1 tsp salt

2 tsp sugar

5 tbsp chopped cashew nuts

3 tbsp chopped fresh coriander

2 tbsp chopped fresh mint

4 green chillies (this may depend on how hot you like it)

slices of lime, to garnish

### METHOD

Put the fish in a bowl and set aside. Using a spice grinder or pestle and mortar, grind all the remaining ingredients together to make a smooth paste. Smear the paste over the fish, ensuring each piece is coated with the herb and nut marinade and set aside for 20 minutes.

Take each piece of fish and wrap in a banana leaf or a piece of foil, sealing securely. Place the fish parcels in a steamer over boiling water and cook for 20 minutes. Keep an eye on the parcels to ensure that none of them open up.

Serve garnished with lime slices.

# Channar Payesh

## Bengali Milk Dessert

SERVES 6

If you truly want to indulge in Bengali sweets, this is a dessert that is little-known outside Bengal. You need to love milky, creamy desserts to really appreciate this! It is served chilled and tastes better if it is made the day before serving. In Calcutta, most people would buy *Channar Payesh* from a specialist sweet shop, where they would cook the milk down in enormous iron pots over coal. After the change in rules, which discouraged burning wood and coal in the city, the sweet shops moved to gas cookers. I still remember the aroma and sounds from my local sweet shop in Calcutta, the smoke from the fire and the sound of the long metal spoon clanging as the *mithai wallah* (sweetmaker) stirred the milk to stop it from sticking to the base of the pan.

### INGREDIENTS

500g *Chenna* (see page 170)

275g caster sugar

50ml water

4 litres full-fat milk

4 green cardamom pods

½ tsp rose water

2 tbsp finely ground pistachios

### METHOD

Make the *chenna* curds according to the method on page 170, then cut the *chenna* into cubes.

Heat 250g of the sugar with the 50ml water, stirring to dissolve the sugar, and boiling until you have a thick syrup. Reduce the heat and add the *chenna* cubes to the syrup, gently stirring so the *chenna* absorbs the syrup. Take the pan off the heat and set aside.

In a heavy-based pan over a high heat, bring the milk and cardamoms to the boil. Reduce the heat and simmer, stirring constantly to prevent the milk from catching at the bottom, until the milk has reduced to half its original volume.

Add the remaining sugar and stir until it dissolves. Then add the *chenna* cubes (and any leftover syrup) and bring the milk back to the boil for 10 minutes, stirring constantly to prevent the milk from burning.

Remove from the heat and leave to cool. Add the rose water and taste for sweetness when it is still slightly warm, adding more sugar to taste. Remember that as the dessert chills, the sweetness will reduce. Sprinkle with the ground pistachios and place in the fridge until completely chilled.

# Thank you

As the book is in her name, I have to start by acknowledging my mother and the pivotal role she played in making me what I am today. My mother's name, Faizana, means 'successful', 'ruler' and 'generosity' – so apt for my Ammu. To my father – Abbu, thank you for giving me the most joyful childhood and teaching me how to appreciate the monsoon rain, music, poetry, the colours of sunrise and the mysterious stars at night. To Amna for being my forever friend, and to my courageous brother Arif, for teaching me how to be positive, brave and kind in adversity. To Ariz and Fariz, thank you for the love.

This book would not have been possible without the incredible work and faith of my literary agent Rachel Conway, who has held my hand throughout the writing process. I also want to thank my Darjeeling Express team, who gave me the time away from work to write this book, especially Eddie, Asha and Julien. I must also mention my husband Mushtaq, not for any contribution he has made to this book or my food journey, but for letting me follow my dream and the path I wanted to tread. He has let me be free to do what I want and not interfered in any of my decisions or choices. For this, I am grateful. Thank you to my mother-in-law, Saeeda Khan, and my sister-in-law, Shaista Khan, for their moral support. Thanks also to Wincie, Maham, and all my cousins, especially Sadia, Sarah and Samreen, for looking after Amna over the years in Dhaka. I am grateful to Asghar Bhaiya, who is now the custodian of the family photographic archives, restoring all the old pictures from my grandfather's and his brother Munna Chacha's collections. Without his help I could not have got all the family pictures of Ammu.

This beautiful book was created and crafted by an amazing team. I have so much love and warmth for all those who worked on it. First of all, the commissioning and in-house editors at Ebury, who believed in this book and gave it life, Laura Higginson and Samantha Crisp. The incredibly patient Emily Preece-Morrison, who never made me feel bad even when I was days late with edits! Laura Edwards (assisted by Jo Cowan and Mathew Hague) captured all the layering of stories and spices in her beautiful photography. As ever, Tabitha Hawkins always had the right prop to hand: the ideal blue plate, or the faded vintage napkin belonging to her grandmother. Tamara Vos (assisted by Jojo Jackson, Charlotte Whatcott and El Kemp) cooked the food to perfection. And, of course, the book's designer, Dave Brown at APE.

Finally, thank you to the copy editor Maggie Ramsay, proofreaders Sarah Epton and Vicky Orchard, and indexer Vanessa Bird. To Lucy Harrison in production at Ebury, and Anjali Nathani, who was responsible for the rights of this book, and to the Ebury crew who worked on getting this book out: Steph Reynolds, Ellie Auton, Francesca Thomson, Alice King, Abby Watson, Morgana Chess, Lara McLeod and Claire Scott.

3

Ebury Press, an imprint of Ebury Publishing,
One Embassy Gardens, 8 Viaduct Gardens,
Nine Elms, London SW11 7BW

Ebury Press is part of the Penguin Random House group of companies
whose addresses can be found at global.penguinrandomhouse.com

Text © Asma Khan 2022
Photography © Laura Edwards 2022,
except images from Asma Khan's private family collection: pages 4, 9, 11,
17, 24 (detail), 27, 28, 44, 45, 55, 72 (detail), 75, 77, 84, 85, 118 (detail),
121, 123, 129, 133, 137, 141, 149, 173, 176 (detail), 179, 180, 185, 196, 207,
234 (detail), 237, 239, 280

Photo corners and edges used on page 4 and throughout © iStockphoto

First published by Ebury Press in 2022

www.penguin.co.uk

A CIP catalogue record for this book is available from the British Library

ISBN 9781529148145

Design: Dave Brown at ape inc. ltd
Photography: Laura Edwards
Food Styling: Tamara Vos
Prop styling: Tabitha Hawkins

Colour origination by Altaimage Ltd, London
Printed and bound in Germany by Mohn Media, Mohndruck GmbH

The authorised representative in the EEA is Penguin Random House
Ireland, Morrison Chambers, 32 Nassau Street, Dublin D02 YH68.

Penguin Random House is committed to a sustainable future for our
business, our readers and our planet. This book is made from Forest
Stewardship Council® certified paper.

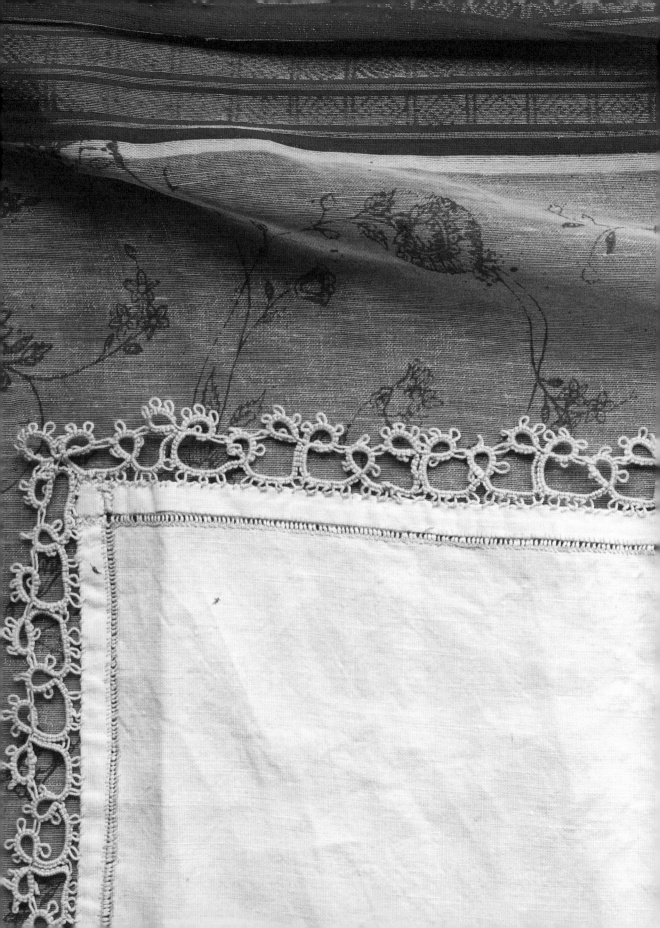